The Light That Changes

The Moon in Astrology, Stories, and Time

by Rhea Wolf

Inner Fire Press
Portland, Ore.
2013

Contents

Acknowledgments

I want to express my deepest thanks and love to Gradey, Scarlet and Madrone for exactly who you are and what you bring to the world.

Thank you to my editing crew: Loren MccRory, Elizabeth Russell and Phyllis Wipf.

Thank you to Gradey for sharing some of your herbal and botanical wisdom.

I have so much gratitude to my mentor and friend Emily Trinkaus, to my collaborator and friend Elizabeth Russell, to my sister in magic Kaylene Beaujolais, to Favor Ellis for all the words and to Jordy Oakland just because.

I want to honor all of my teachers, each of whom still inspire and direct my work: Joanna Macy, Colette Gardiner, Pomegranate Doyle, Sage Goode, Liza Halley and Demetra George.

Big, hearty, loving, gushing, glorious thanks to all those who have provided childcare with pay, without pay, in trade and in service: Denell Graham, Kaliska Sweetwater, Melissa Schaefer, Corinne Wolcott, Nicole Pepper, Corinne D-M, Sam Peterson, Devin Bodeen, Jay Graham, Tamara Wallace, Sarah Canterberry, Maureen Canterberry, Phyllis Wipf, Shawn Zeirdt, Tara DeMaderios, Elyce Brown, Kelli Keegan, Jenni Green Miller and Kaylene Beaujolais.

I am utterly indebted and awed by the brilliant artists who let me include their work in this book: Pomegranate Doyle, Andrea Galluzzo and Iris Leslie.

To the witches who made the story of Asterion come alive, who transformed and blazed a new path with the old story of the Minotaur and the Labyrinth, who gave me a theater experience I have always dreamed of: You are magic. Thank you. You know who you are.

And very special thanks to the woman who helped put this whole book together, using her technical know-how and willingness to learn through doing: Loren MccRory. It has been so much fun to work on this with you.

Dedicated to the ancestors and the future beings.

Introduction
The Queen of Moons

I n 2008, I was reading about the poet and activist Muriel
Rukeyser, wondering how in the hell she managed to write
poems and books while she single-handedly raised a two-
year-old. In the first few years of raising my eldest daughter, I
was lucky if I managed to get a shower in every few days. And she
did it alone, or at least she didn't have a partner in the mix
helping her raise her son. I had a partner and housemates and
friends. I didn't understand in any way, shape or form how this
woman – or any woman, really –finds the time to do their work
while being a mom without some sort of super-human powers or
a large bank account. My own writing never seemed to get
finished. I am not sure that I even know what finished means.

Then a good friend, the amazing astrologer Emily Trinkaus,
emailed me from her office at Tarot.com where she had been

hired as a content writer. Would I be interested in writing an electronic astrology report? Or rather she wrote something like, "You should write this. Now. No excuses."

Emily has done this for me a few times. She's challenged me to live up to my potential. She's believed in me. And for this I am eternally grateful. So I took the challenge. In between breastfeeding and not showering and eating and not sleeping, I wrote an example report of the Moon in Capricorn. I sent it in to the powers that be at Tarot.com. And they liked it. I hired a babysitter and wrote for four hours, two days a week. I wrote when I should have been sleeping. I wrote on the weekends when my partner was around. And yes, I wrote when I should have been paying attention to my sweet, rambunctious, then two-year-old daughter. But it was a lot of fun actually. And I finished it.

Or at least I thought I did. Three years and another child later, my long-time friend and artistic collaborator Elizabeth Russell told me I should write an e-book. I laughed because I wasn't even sure what an e-book was and because writing a book still seemed like an impossible task especially now that I had two daughters to care for. She pushed me, "You can put up that Moon report you wrote for Tarot.com. It's already done. Just add a bit and get it out there."

I dabbled. I stalled. I made excuses. Until finally I thought, "Why not at least give it a try?" I still didn't know exactly what an e-book was, but I decided to write one. I found out my friend Loren MccRory was learning how to publish e-books and self-publish hard copy books at the Independent Publishing Resource Center in Portland. I asked her if she could tell me what an e-book was. She did. I asked her if she could help me publish mine. She said yes.

So she did. Or I did. Here it is. You're reading it. The e-book. And you have my friends to thank (or blame) when you are finished.

I can't believe that I am a mother of two, a professional, a volunteer and a human being, and I finished writing a book. I am not telling you this in order to get your congratulations or kudos. I am telling you this because things happen. And most of the time, they happen slowly, over time, maybe even without your knowing it.

I think most of the good things in my life happened liked this. What I mean is, I struggle and try really hard and think way too much about something, and nothing I want to have happen happens. But when I allow space for connection, open to others' suggestions, watching for subtle signs, and take small steps toward a vision in between all the other responsibilities and duties of living a life, then there's magic. There's something unpredictable. There's something new. A change happens.

The Queen of Moons looks like she understands this: holding a sword and nursing a baby, naked but ready for anything. She is the Moon as mother, protector and guide. She's got a lot going on but still has the look of presence in her eyes. She knows herself, knows she has a lot to do, but greets the changes with poise, strength and love.

This book is called *The Light That Changes* because I really want to understand change. If I could I would put it under a microscope and make a diagram of change with labels and definitions. But that is not the way it works. (Sorry 18th century scientists.) For me, tracking the Moon each month and writing a newsletter that follows the Full and New Moons has been an experiment in understanding change. How does something that happens each year – like summer or the Full Moon in Virgo – offer us something new each time it happens? How do I make the most of this offering?

My own desire to understand change and the way it keeps happening is the soil of this book. The little plants coming up from it are made out of some other desires: the desire for healthy relationships, the desire to listen to my own soul, the desire to tell stories that help us with all of these other desires, the desire for people to see how beautiful and valuable they are (the way I see them). These are some of the ways the Moon can help us better understand ourselves and our world.

I hope that this book meets some of those same needs for you. The Moon is so practical in a lot of ways. Even as it represents the mysterious, kinda witchy, watery depths, it also shows us ways that we can feel comfortable in our own skins on a day-to-day level. It helps us notice our emotions. It helps us choose what to eat, when to plant and how much to sleep. Just take one month out of the year, look at the moon every night, and see for yourself. The Moon's phases are our phases. The Moon's light is our light. And we are little bundles of change.

I want this book to get you in touch with your own light, to support you in embracing who you are, and to help you make the changes you want toward a more authentic life.

How to Read This Book

However you want. You can read it front to back. You can read it sideways. You can read it on a train, in the rain, with a fox, in a box.

But seriously. The first section contains information and stories about the Moon that should be accessible for everyone. You don't need to know anything about astrology to learn something from this section. You'll find stories that delve into themes associated with the Moon and journaling questions to help you make the most of these topics.

In the next section, we'll look at the Moon as it moves through its phases. From New to Full, we'll see how to track the changes and work some personal magic based on which sign the Moon is traveling through. We'll also glimpse the power of eclipses and get a brief overview of the meaning of the lunar phases.

The final section takes us more into the astrology of the Moon. Once you know where the Moon is in your own Natal Chart, you can read all about it here. Each Moon Sign is given a nice round of attention.

For those who want to learn about the Moon through all the signs, houses and aspects, this section is what we in the industry call a "cookbook" because you can look up all the ingredients of the Moon in your friend's/lover's/mother's chart.

Take it one page at a time, front to back, flip around erratically, focus on what you need in the moment. Any way you want it. That's the way to read it. Any way you want it.

Part I. The Moon in Stories

"Myths are things that never happened but always are."

~ Sallustius, Fourth Century Roman poet

The soul, like the moon
by Lal Ded (Lalla)
14th Century Sufi mystic

The soul, like the moon,
is new, and always new again.

And I have seen the ocean
continuously creating.

Since I scoured my mind
and my body, I too, Lalla,
am new, each moment new.

My teacher told me one thing,
Live in the soul.

When that was so,
I began to go naked,
and dance.

Why the Moon Matters

The path that Western culture has taken for the last few hundred years (at least) has attempted to take us closer to the promised land of certainty. If we pull everything apart, measure it, time each moment with excruciating exactitude, the story goes, then we will finally be free from the discomfort of not knowing, the disease of uncertainty.

But of course, this world is wildly unpredictable, surprising us daily with new manifestations of life. Mutations emerge, and with them, chaos inflicts its agenda upon our scheduled order. Sounds dramatic, doesn't it? Well, it is. Our rationally oriented culture has been making big messes and creating drama with its blindness to an essential truth about this thing called life. Namely, that it changes whether we want it to or not.

Heraclitus wrote, "Nothing endures but change." He also said you cannot step into the same river twice. He was a smart guy. Pagans chant, *She changes everything she touches and everything she touches, changes.* The she they are referring to is the Soul of Nature Herself, the life-renewing Great Goddess of the Earth who continually transforms herself and the living planet from maiden to mother to crone and back again. Heraclitus and the pagans know about change.

In our sky, that great heavenly expanse we all share on this precious gem of a planet, the Moon ever reminds us of the truth of change. That is, if we remember to look up and see what's happening. Each month the Moon changes. Contrast this with the Sun, which always appears pretty much the same. The days and nights may vary in length, but that golden solar face varies little. It is the Moon's face that weaves back and forth from dark to full and back again. It is the light that changes.

In many cultures, the Moon was revered over the Sun because its silvery glow appeared when we needed it most – at night. In the darkness, the Moon's glow helped us cope with our fears and see our way through into morning. The constancy of the Sun was seen as less important because it shone during the day, when it was already bright.

This explanation of the order of the Sun and Moon may seem simplistic and irrational, but it holds a deeper truth within it. Of course, we know that the Sun creates the light during the day and the Moon is merely reflecting the light from the Sun. In Jungian psychology, the Sun is seen as the active masculine principle which seeks to assert its will in the world. All light comes from the Sun. Western culture is very solar-oriented and would agree that the Sun is really what's most important to life on earth. From a purely scientific standpoint, this would be true.

Digging deeper into the stories, though, we see that the Moon does offer us the way to move with change and uncertainty, to bring light to the darkness, to bring understanding and peace even in the most painful and challenging of circumstances. The Sun offers its bright constancy. But the Moon offers its mystery.

We human animals are more like the Moon than the Sun in many ways. We may desire stability and constancy but are often at the mercy of unpredictable circumstances – the slings and arrows of outrageous fortune, as Shakespeare wrote. We may wish it weren't so, but as my dad liked to repeat as often as he could, "Wish in one hand and shit in the other, and see which one fills up first."

He has a point. This ride is full of suffering that can't be wished away. How do we cope with it? Reconnecting with symbols that reflect a deeper meaning back into our lives may be one way. The Moon reflects the intensity of the Sun back down to Earth when the darkness is deep and mysterious. Its light is softer and cooler. Its message may be that even in the darkness, there can be a kind of grace that connects us back into the fabric of life.

This may be why those who work closely with the Earth for their spiritual practices offer up more praises to the Moon, why women have felt an affinity for the mysterious Moon which follows them through biological and emotional changes, why tribal cultures have names for each Moon – Wolf Moon, Harvest Moon, Corn Moon – to help us remember exactly where and precisely when we are alive.

We change. We can't help it. Anyone alive who isn't changing is dead, for refusing to change brings in a paralysis of the soul which constricts and imprisons authentic desires deep within, cutting them off from connection. Those who forget how or refuse to change may even be more dead than those whose physical life has ended. For even in dying, our cells, our bones, our tissues are turning back to dust and ash, becoming a part of the great cycle of change that never ceases.

I'm being dramatic again, but I really feel the power of this point: change is always happening. How we move with the changes depends a great deal upon the focus of our lives. If we are focused on cultivating constancy, then we may continually feel bombarded and stressed by the way life moves. If we instead give our focus to our own changing inner rhythms, the self-inside which subtly and not-so-subtly demands every now and then that we chart a course into unknown territory, then we have a better chance at navigating when the shit hits the fan (or fills the hand, if you're still listening to my dad.)

This is the intention behind this book: to broaden our understanding of the Moon in order to discover our own rhythms and thereby create a deeper capacity to move through periods of change. Apparently, it's a book about astrology. But I hope it moves beyond that as well.

I think of astrology as a story. Story is what gives our lives meaning, helps us frame our values. The stories we tell about our world actually determine the shape of the world, the energy and vibrancy of it. As the Jedi Master Obi-Wan Kenobi tells his apprentice in *Return of the Jedi*, "Luke, you're going to find that many of the truths we cling to depend greatly on our own point of view."

Using the tool of story doesn't mean that we ignore the reality of a world that is suffering – the exploitation of earth's resources, the disappearing species, drought in some places and floods in another, peaceful uprising met with violence, all these examples of greed, fear and ignorance that threaten our very existence. It doesn't mean we simply tune those things out and decide to tell a story about how great everything is. (That's called denial.) Rather, using story, we can imbue even painful, terrifying or confusing events with a depth that invites more presence and power in the moment, rather than imbuing these events with more fear, more ignorance, more suffering. We can use story to define our circumstances on our own terms and empower that part of us that knows the way to move with this.

And that is the journey I want to invite you on. Using our knowledge of the story the planets make as they move through the seasonal zodiac, we can possibly understand more of our place here and what needs to be done at this time. I'm interested in providing opportunities for us to use this tool of astrology to decide what we would like to align ourselves with, to use this tool of story to help us create a life of depth and authenticity, to understand what has shaped us thus far and how we might like to see the world in the coming age.

Because most of the time, we don't know what's going to happen next. Life in its entirety – the planets, the elements, the animals, the plants, the whole web of life itself – is so fundamentally complex, it is almost impossible to predict what it will come up with next. The times that we do see the future are moments when we sink in and attune to that unifying intention, when we feel our connection to the pulse of life itself, and even then we just catch glimpses.

Rather than seeking answers about what's going to happen or being attached to things unfolding in a certain way over the next month, year or decade, we can use the symbol of the Moon in astrology and story in order to learn more about inhabiting "states of possibility." Perhaps by looking up at the Moon in the sky and looking within to the inner-Moon, we will catch glimpses of how each one of us can move forward during this time of great uncertainty and still create beauty, respect and love in our own way.

The Moon's Pull

"As above, so below; as within, so without."
~ Hermes Trismegistus

Throughout time, the Moon has been a symbol of deep power and mystery. Legends and sacred stories about the moon have sprouted from every culture, from werewolves whose frightening power is unleashed with the Full Moon, to myths about the love between the Sun and Moon, who chase each other across the sky. We are still enchanted by these tales of love, betrayal and yearning.

The Moon has a story to offer to you as well. Tracking the Moon's phases and the themes that are activated as it passes through the signs of the zodiac can help us find alignment between inner and outer rhythms. Another way we can learn more about who we are and the hidden powers waiting to be discovered within us is by taking a look at where the Moon is in our Natal Charts. Exploring the Moon in these ways can give you a great foundation to understand your true nature and unlock the doors to your desires and needs.

The Moon is often thought of as Feminine in nature. However, this does not mean that its power is only available to folks who identify as women. The archetypal Feminine is simply the part of each of us that is open, receptive, cyclical, changing and mysterious. Everyone, regardless of gender, can experience parts of themselves that are like this.

We are in the realm of the Feminine anytime we feel these qualities at work in our lives. For some of us, our homes may be constantly changing. For others, we may feel more receptive and open in a work environment. And for still others, certain hobbies may connect us to a sense of emotional health or soul-centeredness.

The Feminine is cyclical, which means that it is always changing even as it repeats certain patterns. Just as the Moon creates the tides of the ocean, often there are activities, feelings, people and places that have an inexplicable pull on us, requiring us to repeat lessons and patterns (over and over again) until we find the acceptance or healing we need.

As the moon journeys through its phases, from the ripeness of full to the dark solitude of new, so do we have our own rhythms. These shifting moods can be challenging to navigate, but by learning about this reservoir of power and the core energy it expresses, we can ride our natural cycles so that this power doesn't burst through as destructive behavior.

Stories and Myths of the Moon

The Astrological Moon can give us a glimpse into our specific inner rhythms and emotional needs according to the sign, house and aspects that color its original meanings and expression. But without even knowing anything about astrology or our Moon sign, we can find meaning and insight when exploring the Moon's significance in stories, myths and folktales throughout many different cultures and times in human history.

Often the Moon is a symbol of both light and dark, as well as the interplay between wisdom and states of unknowing. Again, the Moon's light shines when we need it most, when the Sun's rays are missing and darkness threatens to overtake us. And so the Moon becomes a source of comfort, knowledge and safety for those who are awake in the black of night.

The Moon's light is a guide. We can feel a sense of loss when the Moon's light is on the wane, and we can no longer see in the dark. We modern-day humans also feel this loss in our cities where the Moon's light is less obvious. But perhaps most of us notice this less these days. Thanks to electric light, we can conceivably be awake and productive no matter what time it is.

The Moon's productivity is circular and never-ending. As a symbol of the Soul or Deep Self, the Moon doesn't want answers but only more interesting questions to live into. At night, we become more reflective. We dream. We wonder about yesterday's deeds. We worry over tomorrow's expectations. We sleep. We restore ourselves. We contemplate. We relax.

The Moon invites us on a journey of exploration without destination. It wants to show us more and more of what is usually hidden, secret and even confusing. Even though we can feel comfort in its light, we feel too the sense of how small we are in the grand scheme of things, in the vastness of space, and therefore understand how limited we are in seeing the big picture. By the Moon's light, we only see in outlines, ghostly forms and shadows. The circle of the Moon's light is limited by the depth of the darkness.

But darkness is where all life is born. In darkness, we find the beginnings of life: in wombs, in fragile eggshells and in seeds germinating in the earth, life takes hold. Darkness is seen as necessary not only for life to exist, but also for our creativity. Author and Creativity guru Julia Cameron writes:

> "Creativity – like human life itself – begins in darkness. We need to acknowledge this. All too often, we think only in terms of light: 'And the light bulb went on and I got it!' It is true that insights may come to us as flashes. It is true that some of these flashes may be blinding. It is, however, also true that such bright ideas are preceded by a gestations period that is interior, murky, and completely necessary."

In order to create, artists of all kinds must at some point turn their vision toward the within, stay up late, star gaze, feed on the mysterious, and dive into the dark complexities of the human soul. This journey may be undertaken for its own sake or in order to make an offering out into the world of that vision received in the black night.

The dark gives us treasures, just as mines that tunnel deep into the Earth reveal jewels and precious metals. We need the darkness, and we need the silver changing light in the darkness to remind us of how important darkness is to the human imagination and soul.

Stories about the Moon can vary from fanciful myths to ghost stories, from sweet romance to monsters unleashed. The Moon figures heavily in poetry of all kinds. It is the focal point of paintings and the inspiration for songs. The Moon holds something of the numinous. It feels divine. It feels magical. Anyone caught in the gaze of a Full Moon rising through trees, kissing the edges of clouds with gold or silvery threads, can attest to this otherworldly power. It is strange, fantastic and mesmerizing. You can't stare at the Sun like this. You can only sustain such a gaze at the Moon.

In this section, I offer just a taste of the stories that have a lunar resonance for me. Four stories and some thoughts about each one. They may be stories about the Moon, or about a figure associated with the Moon, or just about this certain essential mysterious something that the Moon brings to us in the dark of night. You are invited to read the stories and see what feels resonant, valuable and intriguing to you. I provide some commentary on what the stories mean to me, and there are some questions to help you along the journey at the end of each section.

Bringing Light into the Darkness
The Story of King Minos and Pasiphae

"All myths are public dreams, all dreams are private myths."
~ Joseph Campbell

It is late summer and the skies of Oregon are sunny for a change. A group of women and one man are lounging out on blankets in an open meadow, soaking in the warmth of the light and talking about mythology. What is it? Is it real? Did the gods and goddesses really walk among mortals? Are they only seasonal allegories or explanations of natural or historical events?

This being a group of witches, the answers were less the latter and more the former. As we offered up our own perspectives on how myths and stories work, it was clear that we were definitely pro-myth, myth-centric, biased for stories. For many of us, the eternal stories that are passed down orally and seem to make their way into cultures across the world – while changing a name here or adding a detail there – are truer than histories written down by the scholars. The myths are telling us something eternal while the histories are telling us a certain point of view about certain events, while leaving other events and perspectives out of the picture.

But perhaps myths are prone to this kind of subjectivity as well. Even when eternal truths weave through them, the details and the stories can become distorted so much that we fail to recognize the power at the center. I remember when, in my Teen Sunday School class, it finally dawned on me that humans had actually written the Bible and that the events described therein related to actual historical periods on our planet. Prior to this, I thought that everything in the Bible was somehow instantaneously zapped into existence from on high. I thought that the places being written about were not real places but a kind of never-never land. It was an eye-opening experience to realize that the writers themselves may have had some political and personal stake in the way their stories and myths were recorded.

In the modern world, even the word myth is diminished. It is often used to mean a lie, something not true. "Mythbusters" create whole TV shows to prove that something mystical, magical or unexplainable is actually mundane, false, or explainable. Even when using the word "myth" in its original sense, as a story about gods and goddesses and the creation of things, it is seen as quaint, untrue, a fantasy or superstition. Not real at all.

Myths aren't real, not in the sense that we think of consensual reality. Brushing our teeth. Sitting in traffic. Typing on a computer. Trading stock options on junk bonds. You can't find myths in those kinds of activities (even though the last one sounds totally made up to me.)

The group of us that summer talking about myth and story had been tasked with changing one: the myth of the Minotaur. We were told to find out what really happened. The story the way it had been told had some truth in it, but we weren't interested in that truth. We wanted to move away from the story which had bestiality, betrayal, mass murder and deception at its heart and find the threads in the story about connection, love, surrender and initiation.

We were being asked to change a myth. Thought of in another way, we were being asked to peel back the layers of the myth in order discover something more essential and true, a story that could give us hope in this time.

Each day for three days, we took on a section of the story. We let our imaginations roll over it. We looked at it with our dreaming selves. We took ridiculous events, such as a woman falling in love with a white bull and contracting Daedalus to construct a wooden female bull so the woman could copulate with said white bull. And we wondered, what is this really about?

What could be a deeper truth living within a story that is apparently about fucking animals, giving birth to a monster, locking the monster up in an elaborate maze and offering young maids and lads as meat to the monster every seven years or so?

We had our work cut out for us. But we didn't have a lot of time. We had to re-vision the myth, write a script and then perform it in the evening in front of a large group of our peers and teachers. Our primal instincts had to kick in.

What we ended up with is a story that brought tears to our eyes, love to our hearts and power to our lives. The other story?

The Myth of the Minotaur? You can read that somewhere else if you like. Don't get me wrong. It has its own value. I'm not one to disparage anyone's myths. But what I want to share with you here is a piece of the Story of Asterion, the re-telling we created.

King Minos and Pasiphae

In time so long ago that the rivers and trees and animals still spoke to the humans and the humans still had the ears to hear them, a great king lived in a prosperous land. His name was Minos, and he was not only a king but a man with sacred duties, a priest who worked in concert with the dark earth, the changing seasons and the stars in the heavens, making offerings to the unseen and helping the wheels of creation to turn with beauty.

Every night he gazed upon the Moon with wonder and love. He sang songs to her. He wrote poems to her. He made offerings of honey, wild cypress and wine.

Pasiphae, the Goddess of the Full Moon, looked down upon King Minos with affection as well. She saw the way he honored her, and the oceans, the mountains and the living creatures of earth. One night, as her beauty flowed whole and pure down to the dark earth below, he came to her in deep prayer and asked Pasiphae to join with him.

He spoke, "Oh Pasiphae, shining, brilliant, lovely Full Moon. My beloved. My honey moon. Come to the Earth with me. I love you. Marry me. Become my queen and reign with me. I call you Pasiphae because You are my shining one."

Pasiphae heard his loving prayer and answered, "Promise me that you will honor me, respect me, take care of my ways, and give me what I desire."

King Minos pledged to her his respect and love. He promised to honor her ways. In this way, Pasiphae became both human and goddess, walking the earth with her beloved King Minos.

For years, they lived in happiness, and the kingdom prospered. Pasiphae brought the Moon down to earth, bringing its magic and mystery. She taught the people how to let the Moon shine through their hearts and illuminate their hidden powers. She showed them the power of the Moon to inspire and to create harmonious relationships with each other, with the earth and with the heavens.

But after some time, King Minos noticed how his beloved's own heart grew heavy with longing and grief. She had left her place in the sky, the Full Moon now a light upon the earth. He watched as she gazed up at the crescent moon each month with love and sadness, feeling her loss as his own, a loss of her own pattern and connection.

Because he was a priest and an attentive lover, King Minos could sense all of this, and it troubled him. One night his own worry led him to the ocean. He went down to the ocean and stared out into the waves. He waited at the water's edge until his own heart revealed the words he needed to say.

"By the beauty and power of the ocean, I surrender. I open my heart to you, great mysteries of the waters. My beloved Pasiphae is sick with longing. I don't know what to do. Help me."

King Minos fell to his knees at the water's edge. He let the ocean waves lull him, hold him, caress him. He gazed at the Crescent Moon, hanging there in the western sky like the great silver horns of a pure white bull. As he gazed, the divine power of the ocean opened its arms and drew down the crescent moon as a great white bull. The ocean called the moon down into its mysterious depths.

King Minos watched this like a dream. He saw the White Bull appear like foam on the waves. Graceful and strong, it walked onto the shore, gleaming like starfire. The White Bull walked like a vision out of the ocean and into King Minos' kingdom. Filled with such a stunning vision, the King fell as though he had been struck down, and slept deeply until morning.

Meanwhile, the White Bull found his way to Pasiphae, just as the Crescent Moon in the sky finds the path to its own fullness each month. When Pasiphae saw this lost part of herself, this emissary from her own home, she laughed with joy and abandon. It was like her own heart coming home.

Pasiphae and the White Bull danced together. Slowly at first, and then quicker as if the magnetic pulse of desire commands each action. When at last, they united, something entirely new and unexpected emerged on the earth. The Moon Temple. And the White Bull lived at its heart.

The Moon Temple became a gift for the people, and for all who needed healing, who felt grief and longing, whose hearts were heavy and searching for a way back home. The Moon Temple radiated peace and restoration throughout the land, shining like a beacon to those who had need.

The story goes on to the birth of a precious child, the great god Asterion, half bull-half human, child of Minos and Pasiphae. Asterion brings the magic of dance and the rites of initiation through the path of the labyrinth. But for now we shall leave this story, letting a new take on an old tale fill us with more questions, maybe a little more room to make way for an unexpected miracle or a sweet reunion or an exquisite transformation in our own lives.

How We All Change

In this story, the way to make something new and beautiful requires two ingredients: desire and surrender. The King does this in the beginning, as a priest of the earth who makes the offerings and calls in abundance. He works with the tools of desire and surrender again when he opens his heart to Pasiphae and tells her how he feels about her. If he held anything back, the change would not flow through. His prayers might fall on deaf ears, his own heart might not be able to withstand the outcome of a goddess coming to earth. He might run away in fear. He might walk away in shame or disbelief, thinking his desire is ridiculous, fantastic or unrealistic. But he opens thoroughly. He knows his desire inside and out, and he surrenders to it.

Pasiphae desires to be with him as well and surrenders her old life for something new, to be human and goddess, to be of the heavens and of the earth at once. Maybe it's intriguing to her, the idea of leaving the black sky to walk on feet of flesh and blood and bone. We all seem to be allured by this as well, or we wouldn't keep incarnating and coming back here, now would we?

When finally King Minos realizes the suffering that accompanies Pasiphae's change, he goes to the ocean to pray for Pasiphae. That's really what he's doing. He is led to the ocean by the knowledge that often there is some suffering that accompanies any change. He knows suffering in his own life as well, one can imagine. The pain of being human, of enduring confusing feelings and messy interactions that fall short of our dreams and visions. We all know this suffering, don't we? When we are on our knees, when we can't take anymore, even those who don't believe in prayer may find themselves whispering a little "help!" out to the universe, hoping maybe someone will hear.

In this story, the Divine does hear King Minos. We can think of what happens next in two ways. In the first, the Divine hears him, comes down to earth as a bull, and Pasiphae has sex with the Bull. This is closer to the original telling of the Greek myth, where the wife of King Minos is fiercely hot for a White Bull that is to be sacrificed for Poseidon.

But the other way to think of this may be that the Divine, which is always alive within us, hears our prayers. And we receive grace. Grace is a moment of awakening. It is the road made a bit easier by an understanding or revelation that takes us out of our usual perceptions and into a place of depth. Grace is suddenly seeing the truth, and it often comes when we remember our shared connections with each other. When we reach out to tell someone how we feel. When we fall on our knees at the ocean, telling it our secrets like a good friend. When we read a book about someone else going through something real and hard and beautiful, and this story gives us a glimpse of how to move through. Whenever we remember we are somehow inexplicably yet irrevocably connected to the larger fabric of life, we receive such grace. And yet another change is initiated.

So when King Minos falls to his knees, it is his love for Pasiphae that demands that he surrender. When the White Bull appears, it is coming to remind Pasiphae of something that she also must surrender to. I don't know what that is for her. Maybe it's a feeling of regret for her choice to come to earth. Maybe it's her confusion of being human and divine. Maybe it's her longing for children. Whatever it is, she dances with it – the part of herself she left behind. She dances with it, unites with it, and by this union something new is created.

We are changing all the time, even when we don't recognize it. Often, all it takes is recognition and we are moved into sudden joy or acceptance. This new story of King Minos and Pasiphae illuminates this theme of change as we make our personal journeys to the Moon. It tells us, like so many philosophers of old, that all we are *is* change. That we can never step in the same river twice. That the only constant is change. That she changes everything she touches. That we have to be the change we want to see in the world.

If I am running this point into the ground, it is for a good reason. When we open to change, to the dance of surrender and desire, our lives become better. It's not even that they necessarily become different. Our lives may stay pretty much the same circumstantially. But if we have made the leap to awareness that we are always changing, we make way for grace and acceptance to move into us.

The Moon in the sky is change. That may be the most essential thing it teaches us. Change happens. Look up at the Moon and be reminded that it's okay. Change is happening all the time. And it actually makes the world turn. It is what we came here to do.

Some of my witch pals and I changed a story late last summer. And it has made a huge shift in our lives. When we performed the sacred drama, we recognized how both desire and surrender are necessary for authentic self-expression. Going forth with our new understanding of change and a little bit of the Moon Temple in our hearts, each of us has undergone profound transformation in our personal lives, making it possible to take risks, ask for what we really want and, eventually, to get it. Even with the eternal, there is always more to be revealed.

Journaling Questions: Desire and Surrender

In your own life, what events, experiences or moments have been the most profound?

In general, how do you feel about change? Are you a change junkie, looking for something new around every corner? Or do you prefer to stay the course and settle into comfortable patterns?

What does surrender mean to you? When have you had to give up?

There is a prayer in certain paths of witchcraft that goes, "I would know myself in all my parts." Write about what this phrase means to you. What does self-knowledge have to do with desire? Author and earth-activist Joanna Macy poses a question in her book *Coming Back to Life* that goes something like this: "What would you be doing if you knew you could not fail?" Answer it. What gets in the way of making the changes you desire?

What stories from your past might be ready for a new take, a fresh perspective or an innovative retelling? Make a list of old stories from your life. Pick one and write about it in a totally new way. It's okay to make it up. It's okay if it feels like a lie. It's okay if you think the new story is ridiculous. Just do it and see what shifts for you.

Time for Rest and Reflection
The Story of Hina, Hawaiian Moon Goddess

The story of Hina is a traditional Hawaiian tale that explains the pattern on the surface of the Moon, but also informs us of essential lunar rites that we must observe in order to maintain optimum balance and health. Namely, there is a time for work and a time for rest.

When our story begins, Hina is already a grandmother, so old that no one can remember a time when she wasn't around. She tends her gardens and gives to humanity from the hala and kukui trees. She watches over the children and grandchildren and great-grandchildren, singing them songs and teaching them stories that will help them remember what is important in life. She is a hard worker, strong and capable. Everyone relies on Hina for some kind of nourishment, whether it is literal or soulful.

Her husband is old, too, but instead of embodying a wise man, he is a cantankerous fool. He is a lazy man who contributes very little to the household. He goes out fishing in the morning but expects Hina to gather what he has caught, prepare his dinner and clean his boat for him each night. He does this without gratitude or even consciousness of all that she does every day.

But one day, after so many years of ceaseless labor, Hina starts to dream of finding somewhere that she can simply sleep, relax and let go of all her duties. As she dreams of this, she whispers her wish into the world, and the spirits hear her.

Any wish that is spoken gives the Powers That Be a chance to engage with us in the dance of life. Our word is a way of making desire manifest. Magic often happens through the speaking of incantations or prayers, and even most creation stories begin with the speaking of a word or the singing of a song. As Hina whispers her wish into the world, she is letting the gods know that she is ready for change. No more dreaming, time to take action.

Because this story happens in the space of "once upon a time," support from unseen and unusual places is always at the ready. The winds hear her. The rainbow hears her. The light hears her. The rains hear her. They begin to move together toward tending Hina's dreams.

One day she is napping with one of her many great-grandchildren when her husband pops up unexpectedly and shakes her awake. He pulls the child off her lap and tells her to "get to work."

Hina gets up and slowly walks over to her lush gardens. The breeze blows, the light changes, and a soft mist begins to envelope her. She feels the coolness of the water on her skin. As she bends over to pull some weeds out of the ground, she falls as if taken over by the tiredness of her bones. She falls and rolls onto her back. She relaxes into the earth and feels it support her. Looking up into the skies, she sees a rainbow slowly descending down, reaching toward her.

She rises up to get a clearer look at the beautiful threads of color weaving across the sky, and hears it speaking to her. The rainbow tells her, "We have heard your prayers. Climb up the rainbow bridge to find a place to rest." She sees that the band of blue on the rainbow is a path, and she touches its solidness with her hands.

The sun appears now, but from behind the clouds, and she feels its sweet warmth going deep into her bones. She begins to climb, climb, climb, up into the sky. She thinks it would be nice to rest in the Sun. She imagines the warmth of the Sun easing her aching bones. She imagines drowsing in the lazy afternoon glow every day. Each step takes her closer to the sun, and each step brings greater heat and anticipation.

But as she nears the place where the sun lives, the heat grows intolerable. This is not the warm and gentle place of her dreams, a place where she could rest in comfort. The heat of the sun burns her skin and makes her hair frizzle-fried.

At the top of the rainbow, she decides to go back down again. The sun is not welcoming to her. Disappointed and tired from her long trek up, she walks down to earth and finds that it has taken her all day to make the journey.

It is dark in her garden now. She walks slowly to her house and tends to the blisters on her skin and the damage to her hair. She washes her body and rubs lotions onto her skin, letting the coolness revive her.

In the distance, she hears a grumbling sound and knows that it is her husband complaining. She says to herself, "He'll be wondering where I went to, why there is no supper on the table, why there is no water from the well. Well, I will let him grumble a little longer."

Hina looks up to the sky again. The silver crescent moon has risen in the east, bringing a soft light to everything. Hina basks in the sweet night's magical atmosphere.

Speaking to herself, to the night air, to the gods, to no one, she considers making the Moon her new home. "The light of the Moon is cooler and gentler than the Sun's light. Perhaps the Moon would be a good place to rest."

The rainbow hears her again. It stretches down its path to her. Once more, Hina begins to climb on the band of blue color up toward the sky.

Before she has climbed a few feet, her husband's harsh voice breaks through silence.

"Oh no, you don't! There's too much work to be done. Where have you been anyway? Come back here!" he shouts to her. He lunges for her and grabs one of her feet. But Hina is determined. She struggles against his grip and with a great *crack!* she frees herself. Her husband falls with a thud to the ground, still complaining and yelling at her to come back.

Hina's foot is hurt from the fight, but she hobbles on. Up the blue path to the Moon, who welcomes her with a kind, soft and gentle light. The crescent of the Moon is shaped like a hammock, and Hina climbs in for a good, long rest.

And there she is still. If you look up, you can see her resting there. Only now she is called Mono-Loku.

Taking Care

There are times when we can be ignorant or resentful of the Moon inside of us. Maybe it should be obvious that we need to take care of our feelings and our bodies and take time to rest. But so often, we simply don't.

Not noticing how much our bodies do for us, we race from one obligation to the next, grabbing a mouthful of whatever's handy and another cup of coffee. Meanwhile, we are depleting our natural strength and resiliency by missing out on the sleep and nourishment we need.

The husband in the story is both reproachful of his wife taking too much time to rest while simultaneously embodying the kind of irresponsibility that borders on complete inertia. He does not feel responsibility to anything. The word "responsibility" sounds a lot like "response-ability" to me. Our ability to respond means two things: responding to and honoring our obligations and duties in this life and responding to and honoring our own limitations and boundaries. When we are like the husband, we are unaware of both.

Sometimes we keep walking toward the sun, thinking that we will rest once we accomplish a project or finish a goal we've set for ourselves. The sun represents our outer world accomplishments. If we rely too much on those accomplishments to determine how and when we will give back to ourselves, we will often burn out.

Learning how to balance and restore the Feminine in our world means taking time out of every day to rest, reflect and replenish our personal power and resources. Hina teaches us that our strength and endurance comes out of our ability to relax and feel support from those around us. It is important to take time to appreciate what your body does for you, and to feel gratitude for what you do to take care of yourself.

Nurturing Ourselves: Journaling Questions

Take some time to reflect on these themes and questions in your journal or in your mind.

Taking care of ourselves can be easily folded into the activities we already perform every day. What we eat, how we bathe our bodies, what we wear, how we get our exercise – any of these things can be imbued with a sacred or loving intention that brings us more fully into our bodies. When we are present with our bodies and emotions, we are more aware of what we require for our health and what our health requires of us.

Are there rituals you do for yourself that feel healing, nurturing or re-charging?

What activities make you feel supported in the work that you do?

How much sleep do you know you need? How much do you usually get? What are the things that keep you from getting this amount of sleep?

Do you pay attention to the Moon in the sky? Do you notice a relationship between the changing phases of the moon and your own energy levels?

How do you talk to yourself? Are you an inner bully or a bit passive?

What is the connection between your outer world accomplishments and your inner world desires? Are they in agreement?

Restoring Desire
The Story of Artemis and Actaeon

The Moon can be a symbol of domestic life: hearth and home, relationships and daily life. But it also speaks to us of wilderness and instinct. In ancient Greece, the Goddess Artemis was lunar in nature and also queen of the wilds. As a protector of all wild places and animals, she represented instinctual knowing and the shared connections between plant, animal and human. As a hunter, she knew the mystery rites of killing, the necessity of death in creating the cyclical order of life.

In her stories, she regularly returns to her sacred waters in order to be cleansed and purified, to restore herself to a sacred, pure state of consciousness. This could come from an understanding that hunters – even goddesses - who take life are changed in a fundamental way. A period of purification is then required in order to rebalance the energies within, to assimilate the experience of darkness without letting it take over completely. To do this, Artemis visits her sacred waters and bathes, naked and humble.

One day, a young man named Actaeon is out in the forest on a hunting expedition. While chasing a great stag, he wanders away from the rest of his hunting party. As he nimbly tracks the deer through the trees, he hears something stir in a small clearing. Thinking he has the animal out in the open, he prepares for a good shot as he quietly approaches the glen. What he finds is Artemis, Goddess of the Wilds, naked and bathing in her sacred waters.

Actaeon is transfixed. He does not turn away. Never has he seen such a beautiful sight. The goddess' beauty is astonishing, but so is her absolute attention to letting the waters wash her. Actaeon senses humbleness, vulnerability and also power. His desire for Artemis grows strong. He stares compulsively at the goddess' nakedness. His body moves toward her, filled with instinctual desire. Hearing the sound of someone approaching, Artemis turns toward the noise and sees Actaeon brazenly and foolishly coming toward her.

Artemis' rage is palpable. No one lays eyes on the goddess bathing in her sacred waters without facing the consequences. The goddess speaks a curse on Actaeon. She forbids him to tell anyone of what he has seen and further, she warns him to never speak again or more dire consequences will await him. Really, he's getting off easy.

Dumbfounded – literally - Actaeon wanders back into the forest to look for the rest of his hunting party. He hears the distant call of his dogs and suddenly forgets the curse pronounced upon him just moments ago. He excitedly calls out in hopes that someone will hear him and rescue him from his recent shock. But as soon as he opens his mouth, the rest of Artemis' curse is activated. Actaeon is turned into a stag. His own hunting dogs are quickly in pursuit, not recognizing their former master. After a short chase, the dogs capture and kill Actaeon, tearing him to pieces.

Actaeon could represent unconscious desires that often lead us into mysteries we may not fully understand. Actaeon accidentally stumbles upon the Moon Goddess undergoing her mystery rites. This is not something you see every day. He is a bit ignorant of what he is witnessing and yet unable to stop himself from going further.

Actaeon's very human instincts take over. Had he been humbled by the power of witnessing a goddess performing a sacred rite in his presence, he may have had the wisdom to quietly sneak away. But his desires get the best of him.

This is the arrogant side of power, which seeks to know more and claim more than we may be ready for. When we are in the presence of the truly awesome, we may feel humbled or we may seek to claim this power for ourselves somehow. The small self may not know what it's getting into; it only wants what it sees. This ego-driven action leads to the transgression.

When Artemis sees him, it is surprising that she doesn't incinerate him on the spot. Maybe because she is in the lunar waters of healing and purification, her more forgiving side comes to the surface. In some stories, Actaeon is actually a friend of hers, which may explain why she showed some restraint. She gives Actaeon an out. Don't talk. Let yourself be silent. Come to your senses and get back to your inner rhythm. The loss of speech she imposes could be a kind of purification. And it's also a choice. She doesn't take the power of speech from him. She simply says, "Be quiet now. If you aren't, you'll be sorry."

Remaining silent could have possibly restored Actaeon to his wits, gotten him back in touch with his healthy desire and instincts. If he allowed his silence to purify him, perhaps he would have undergone a transformation to help him understand the true power of what he had witnessed. Instead, he called out to the old and familiar and so was transformed in another way, physically changed into an animal. Perhaps he was too afraid to assimilate the experience. Perhaps he was truly just a fool who never knew what was good for him. The Moon is, after all, a symbol of what the soul requires in order to be balanced and healthy.

In Greek mythology, Artemis is eternally a virgin. She never wished to marry but to remain free and wild in her own domain. And yet Artemis is also a goddess who would call young lovers to the forest for moonlit orgies. Who's to say if a free and wild goddess wouldn't let her virginity slip once in a while?

So she goes to the waters to be restored. Both sex and hunting change one and mingle one's essence with another's. If we are to remember our true nature, we must undergo a purification, not to forget the experience or wash away the relationship with another, but to integrate it into our own experience. We cannot lose ourselves so entirely that we walk into dangerous situations, such as the unwitting Actaeon did. He wanders out of the ordinary reality and into a place of power. He is forgetful of the proper observations to make when this happens and unaware of the danger in his own desires. If he knew himself, he might have known better than to wander too close to the site of Artemis' power. Not knowing with his intellect, he could have felt intuitively that he was approaching something taboo, in this case a place where you must have a sacred purpose in order to enter.

The original meaning of virgin was simply "unwedded," and some writers of the women's spirituality movement have uncovered that this designation may have had more to do with matrimony than sexual chastity. In many ancient cultures, a woman's way out of marriage was to go into a life of service, becoming a priestess. Some roles of the priestess involved healing, settling disputes, feeding and housing those in need and tending the sacred rites, including those of the sacred prostitute who would initiate others into the sacred mysteries of sex.

If we follow this thread, then the Virgin is not necessarily about denying sexuality, but about belonging to one's self. Artemis needs to bathe in the waters to remember herself, to return to a state of essential beingness. As I said earlier, in other versions of this myth, Actaeon was actually a friend and hunting companion of Artemis until he desired to make her his consort. Actaeon overstepped the bounds of the relationship, whether by intruding and staring at the goddess or by trying to claim something that was not his. Perhaps if Actaeon knew more about his own desires and took action from a sacred rather than a compulsive and unconscious place, he would not have met such a violent fate, torn apart by his own animals (instincts).

Artemis can teach us how to have sovereignty over the realms of our own inner wilderness. She can teach us about our own passions and instincts, even when we over-reach into territories we have no right or claim to. Just as the Full Moon shines down on us and whips us up into a kind of lunacy, we have to be able to cut loose every now and then while maintaining appropriate boundaries. Perhaps it is all about intention. In this case, the respect one maintains for oneself as well as others is what really matters.

Some cultures employ useful ceremonies of wantonness and abandon so that these unseemly behaviors don't leak out all over the rest of the year and cause havoc in our lives. What if we allotted some time to go crazy to keep us from going truly insane?

Undertaking the commitment to understand the dark and hidden places within us clears the way to assert ourselves and take decisive action on the stage of our lives. When we fail to take time considering the nature of desire or why we are drawn to a certain person, place or thing, we can end up acting out without respect for self and others. We can be curious about the unconscious depths, the unseen forces within and around us, but we must approach this territory mindfully or we could wind up getting torn to bits. Even if we screw up and our lives implode, Artemis can show us the way to restore ourselves with beauty, silence and respect for self.

Exploring Desire: Journaling Questions

In considering this story, we see the themes of unconscious desires and passions, the need for purification, and the call to reclaim one's instincts or intuition. To explore these themes in your own life, use the prompts and questions below.

Although they are sources of power and creativity, passion and desire can also turn into obsessions and lead us into trouble. What are your passions? What are your obsessions?

Like Actaeon, are there parts of yourself that frighten or overwhelm you? These could be desires, powers or skills you have, or even people or events in your life. Make a list about the frightening and the overwhelming.

What about the world is compelling, mesmerizing and intriguing to you?

What do you do when you need to cut loose? Do you notice feeling a little wild when the moon is full?

Just as Artemis cleanses in the sacred waters in the heart of her wilderness, we have parts of ourselves that need to be restored and purified. What gets in the way of your instincts and desires?

What do you do when you need to clear your perception or form a new perspective on something?

What actions help you restore and renew your instincts after you make a mistake or take a wrong turn in life?

The Sun and Moon Chasing Each Other
Stories of Balance and Imbalance

There are many folk tales and regional myths about why and how the sun and the moon share the same sky. In one from West Africa, the sun and the moon correspond to male and female deities who are lovers. The Fon people believed the Sun was a fierce warrior god named Liza and that the Moon was the healing goddess of creation named Mawu. In tales from this tribe, they are both responsible for keeping the balance of the universe in check, and in those rare times when the sun and moon meet for a solar eclipse, Mawu and Liza are making love.

In other cultures, the story is not so loving and bright. In Japan, the Moon and Sun have a more tumultuous relationship. In the beginning, the solar goddess Amaterasu shared the sky amicably with her brother-husband the Moon, known as Tsukuyomi. But one day, Tsukuyomi killed the Goddess of Food because her actions were repulsive to him. From that point on, Amaterasu would have nothing to do with her brother. But he still chases his sister the Sun in order to apologize for his crime.

One tale from the Inuit cosmology also reports that the Sun is continually chased by the Moon seeking forgiveness. Malina and Anningan are sister and brother. One night, Anningan forces himself on his sister. Malina cannot see who it is that has raped her because it is totally dark out. But the next night, she is ready in case her attacker returns. Before bed, she smears her hands in the ashes from the fire. When Anningan comes to her again, Malina takes her hands and smears them on his face. In the morning light, she can see that it is her own brother who has violated her.

Anningan realizes that he has been caught and also realizes what he has done. He goes to Malina to ask for forgiveness. But Malina wants nothing to do with him. She flees from him. Anningan follows the trail of blood she leaves behind so he may apologize to her. He chases her and she flees. They move so quickly that their speed carries them up to the sky, where Malina becomes the Sun, for her courage, strength and beauty, while

Anningan becomes the moon, with ash-smeared face, continually seeking the forgiveness he never receives.

This story may seem especially dark and painful, but it contains important information for us in our lunar journey. Each human carries wounds and traumas as serious as the ones endured by Malina, although the circumstances and events are unique to each of us. Sometimes these wounds come from people especially close to us. The Moon can represent our family experiences and ancestral ties, the people and stories that need healing and eventually maybe even forgiveness. When we are consciously tending our lunar nature, we will seek out people and places that can support us in our own healing from past experiences. Being aligned with the Moon here does not mean agreeing with or excusing the actions of an aggressor. But it does seem that the real healing the Moon has to offer us comes from facing the dark spots of the past in order to move forward in wholeness.

The Moon is not just representative of the family complex, but also the complex web of our inner lives. Sometimes the perpetrator of horrible deeds comes from inside of us. Sometimes we betray ourselves and violate our own bodies, hearts and minds. When this is the case, it takes all of our courage to face the onslaught of attacks and learn how to stop the abuse. This may mean taking action to stop others from abusing us or stealing our power. It may mean stopping ourselves from continuing to harm or violate ourselves. Self-abuse leads to a wide range of unhealthy and even destructive behaviors, from alcohol and substance abuse, to food addictions, dangerous sexual activity, self-hurting and even self-mutilation.

In my own life, it took years for me to even face my experiences of sexual violation. Once I did, it seemed easy for me to forgive my rapist and others who had misused their power against me. Much more challenging and painful was the process of forgiving myself. I blamed myself for a variety of choices and actions that led me into dangerous situations. I blamed my lack of awareness. I scolded myself for not taking action sooner. I chastised my younger self for being so reckless, so stupid. Instead of healing from the pain, I chose to numb it in a variety of ways.

Finally, I realized that numbing out the pain was simultaneously numbing out joy, love and my own power. Once I could begin to accept what had happened to me and forgive myself for not being able to stop it, I began to regain my full range of emotions. Eventually, I felt my own power and authority returning as well, enabling me to make choices in alignment with both my blazing light and my rich darkness.

Following the trail of blood – the damage that we have suffered – we can eventually find forgiveness. Though the Inuit story does not go on to tell us of New Moons or Eclipses when the two siblings may meet again, we can continue the story in our own lives to find a way to deal with the fallout of painful and traumatic experiences.

Whenever the Sun and Moon meet, we are blessed with a New Moon, a time which symbolizes beginnings. With each New Moon, we can set intentions, let go of the past and call for healing. The Sun in astrology and mythology is a symbol of our own courage, strength and the destiny we came here to live out. When it aligns with the Moon astrologically, as with the New Moon conjunction each month, we have a chance to see the ways our inner worlds and outer worlds meet. We check in with the inner world, pay attention to what our bodies and hearts truly need to thrive, write down some intentions, and make adjustments in how we live.

We may seek out brighter futures for ourselves by forgoing any journeys into the darkness, but we will always feel weighed down by life if we do not acknowledge the mysterious realms within us. It takes courage to recognize that throughout life we may play the role of both victim and aggressor. If we take the healing that the Moon offers, then we have to accept forgiveness for all the ways that we hurt ourselves and one another. I'm not suggesting that this is easy. But it is part of being human.

Forgiveness: Journaling Questions

The Moon within each one of us holds complexity and mystery. As a keeper of memory, the Moon holds painful experiences from our past as well as deep longings that go unfulfilled.

What experiences from your past have you had to heal from? How do the themes and/or people associated with these experiences continue to appear in your life?

What are the ways you violate or disrespect your own body, heart, mind or spirit? How have these experiences helped you cope with or flee from your pain?

What does forgiveness mean to you? Is it necessary to forgive in order for healing to happen?

What do you need to forgive yourself for?

Part II. The Moon in Time

Such a slender moon, going up and up,
Waxing so fast from night to night,
And swelling like an orange flower-bud, bright,
Fated, methought, to round as to a golden cup,
And hold to my two lips life's best of wine.

~ Jean Ingelow (1820-1897)

E ach monthly Moon cycle brings with it a chance to change. The Moon is our most visible reminder of the on-going process of giving birth to ourselves. Each month, there are those few nights when the sky is pitch black and seems empty, even with the twinkling of stars peering through the dark veil of space. And then there comes a night when we see the delicate sliver of light hanging low on the horizon, and our hearts fill with wonder at the sight. Such a fragile silver crescent, but such a potent symbol of beginnings.

It's the same in our own lives. When we are about to move into new territory, when we sense that a deep change is about to appear on the horizon, it can feel dark, cold and empty in the world. We feel lost, as though something is dying inside, and are often confused about how we will ever make it through. When the moon is dark and hidden, we are too. Our dreams and visions turn within as we sort out the messages of our own souls.

Listening to the darkness and the well of feelings within us, we can hear the voice of our deeper self. As our awareness flows to the deep self, some part of our essence brings forth an old pain to be healed or a new feeling to be shared. Once we understand what our inner-voice is trying to tell us, it may not get easier – not right away – but we can at least begin to move forward with intention.

When the New Moon occurs every month, we all have a chance to move out of the darkness and into focus. The New Moon is the time to set intentions for where we want to go. It is the time to decide what we'd like to call into our lives. It's an opportunity to cleanse and open our vision wider to new potentials.

In our modern lives, many of us can't even see the stars from the incessant glare of city lights, and often we don't pay attention to the fluctuating shape of the Moon. But almost every calendar these days shows us the dates for the Full and New Moons. Even if we aren't looking into the sky, we can look into ourselves and align with the rhythms of the dark and the sweetness of the new.

The New Moon itself is a time for renewing and inspiring whatever currently needs our attention. Knowing the sign that the New Moon is in each month can help us go even further in creating intentions with power and purpose. The special themes related to each sign of the Zodiac tap us into specific energies that we can utilize to craft our most heartfelt wishes and intentions.

Intentions are different than goals. A goal is some fixed idea of an endpoint we'd like to reach, such as the finish line of a race. Goals are good for accomplishing certain tasks, but there are times when goals can trick us out of seeing what is actually best for us, especially in relationship to our inner work. When we have a goal, we expect a certain outcome, like finishing the race, getting a certain job or moving to a certain place.

Intentions leave room for the wish to unfold in surprising ways. Instead of a tape hanging off in the distance waiting for the racers to break through, intentions are the very ground we tread upon in each moment.

Setting goals usually requires that we hold firm to an image, date or desired outcome in our minds. But an intention holds us. In this way, we don't have to know where we are going all the time but rather just know what is currently important on our path. *What is valuable to my journey right now?*

Maybe we don't know what the perfect job for us is, or who the perfect partner might be, or even where we want to live. With intentions, we are careful to phrase them in such a way that we are open to however the journey unfolds while being specific enough to get what we need.

For example, let's say I need a change in my work – I'm not making enough money; I'm feeling dissatisfied about the type of work I do; I am not getting recognized for my accomplishments. So I might create an intention that states, "I will easily find work that utilizes my unique skills and passions, and supports me financially, emotionally and spiritually." (I can even add in what those unique skills and passions are, as long as I don't name the job I think I should have. This would limit my perception.)

My part of the bargain in this intention-making is to tend this intention every day. I might say it to myself when I wake up or when I look in the bathroom mirror to brush my teeth. I might even fold it into my spiritual practice, make a collage about it, or build an altar to hold it.

You know how to build an altar? You set aside a table, space on the floor, or a shelf. Then you imagine that energy that you want to call in. Next, you wander around your house, apartment or neighborhood, letting objects grab your attention. Whatever objects, animals, colors you notice are telling you they can help. So you put them – or an image of them – on the altar. The altar helps you remember your intentions. It holds the space and reminds you of what you are doing in your life so that even if you don't notice the changes, you can find trust that they are happening.

When I make an intention, I am committing to pay attention. I am telling the universe that I will notice my life. What experiences, seemingly random occurrences or thoughts come up for me? Each day, I will visit my altar, look at the collage, say my intentions or do some small action that reminds me that I am changing. Every day, I practice letting go of certainty and opening to possibilities. In this way the intention can show me the way to move forward. Unlike goals, I don't have to already know where I'm headed to get there.

I always like to put an addendum on my intentions and wishes that states, "this or something better," as it acknowledges my own current limitations of perspective and gives it over to the goddess (which you might call universe, god, higher power, creator, etc.).

Don't worry if you think you don't know how to make intentions. In the following pages, you'll find plenty of topics related to each sign to help you get in sync with the energies of each New Moon. The month in which you can expect each New Moon in a certain sign is given, although the precise dates will vary from year to year.

New Moon Intentions

Intentions compressed into words enfold magical power.

~ Deepak Chopra

The moment one definitely commits oneself then providence moves too. All sorts of things occur to help one that would never otherwise have occurred... unforeseen incidents, meetings, and material assistance, which no man could have dreamed would have come his way.

~ Goethe (from various translations)

Aries

♈

New Moon Invocation
Beginning Again

Occurs each year when the Sun is in Aries
(March 21 - April 19)

Aries is the first sign of the Zodiac, the sign of spring and new beginnings. Aries bursts with life, bringing the vital pulse of the Earth up from the ground and into the light. New Moon Intention-Queen, Jan Spiller, says that this New Moon is the most powerful of the whole year. It is an especially strong time to create your own wish list of things you'd like to accomplish in the year ahead.

Aries is the sign of the ram running headfirst into the heat of battle. Archetypes associated with Aries are the Pioneer, the Warrior and the Eternal Teenager. With the New Moon in Aries, we have the opportunity to forge a new path, to summon our strength and power in service to our desire and will.

You can think of this New Moon as a New Year of sorts. We are fully facing the spring and feeling our own life force begin to awaken. We begin to focus on what we want to accomplish after the quiet of winter.

Specific intentions for this New Moon can focus on areas ruled by Aries, such as:

- Trusting your impulses
- Cultivating authenticity
- Beginning new projects
- Taking action on a project
- Making positive changes to your appearance and/or style
- Stepping into leadership roles
- Beginning a new program of physical activity, sports or exercise
- Discovering an inner appreciation for your ideas, skills and/or physical appearance

- Eliminating selfishness and arrogance
- Working with anger, impatience, rage or emotional impulsiveness
- Creating healthy boundaries that support you
- Engaging in healthy competition
- Connecting to your inner teenager to heal, remember or revitalize
- Working toward healthy expressions of your sexuality
- Healing for headaches, head/face and brain issues

The Queen of New Moon Astrology, Jan Spiller, says that this is the most powerful New Moon of the year for making wishes and setting intentions. Take advantage of this power to set a new course or spend more time doing what you truly love by reflecting on your hopes and desires for this light-filled part of the year.

Taurus

New Moon Invocation
Stability

Occurs each year when the Sun is in Taurus
(April 20 - May 20)

Taurus is the sign of the bull and is cautious, slow and strong by nature. A New Moon in Taurus invites us into our senses, exploring the pleasures of the body and the beauty of the living Earth. Use the energy of this New Moon to call in abundance, fertility and the energy of stability into your life.

Taurus is one of the signs ruled by Venus, the Goddess of Love. Here, she is the goddess of the lush, living Earth, inviting us to see the spiral of life – birth as well as death – and find peace. With the New Moon in Taurus, we are invited to consider what we are attached to. This can show us what our values are, the things we love beyond all reason. And it can also show us where we might be stuck and mired in a situation that needs to change. Is it time to let go of old habits and find new ways of creating health, happiness and wellness in your life?

This New Moon can help us find the determination and perseverance to pull through challenging life circumstances and come out stronger. Perhaps there are areas of your own life that could use the force of the Bull to get things done.

Specific intentions for this New Moon can focus on areas ruled by Taurus, such as:

- Cultivating sustainability in your life
- Creating stability and peace in work, relationships, and home
- Focusing on gardens and food production
- Resolving issues with or providing healing for animals and pets
- Cultivating a healthy body image
- Inviting more sensual pleasure into your life
- Stepping out of emotional and physical ruts (depression, inactivity, over-indulgence)
- Inviting in material and financial security
- Releasing fears and issues of scarcity
- Letting go of control issues and stubbornness
- Finishing projects
- Healing for throat, neck and voice

Gemini

♊

New Moon Invocation
The Power of Connection

Occurs each year when the Sun is in Gemini
(May 21 - June 20)

Gemini is the sign of the twins and is inquisitive, social and flexible by nature. With Gemini, we seek to branch out and discover new ways of perceiving the world. Use the energy of this New Moon to call more curiosity into your life and to see the connections between different ideas, people, or places. Perhaps there are connections to discover within you as well.

The Greek God Hermes is associated with Gemini. In myth, Hermes was the winged messenger who could freely travel between all the worlds, even the underworld. Mercury can help us find freedom of movement as well when our thoughts, bodies, feelings or spirits have become too rigid. With the New Moon in Gemini, we break out of limitations. We step into places that promise new insights about our inner life.

Mercury, the ruling planet of Gemini, also oversees the free-flow of commerce and the news of the day. We can call on Hermes/Mercury to help us whenever we need to know what's going on, to free up flows of information or commerce, and to gain safe passage through both inner and outer worlds.

As the sign of communication and language, Gemini will help us perceive ourselves and the world in new ways by coaxing out stories that need to be told and retold. Sometimes naming something for what it is allows healing to happen. And sometimes the story has to be seen from a new point of view before healing can happen.

With the New Moon in Gemini, consider which area in your life could use a new point of view. Are there people, activities or places that you have always been curious about? This Moon invites us to examine how we use our skills of communication. Is it to investigate and uncover – or to confuse and mislead?

Specific intentions for this New Moon can focus on areas ruled by Gemini, such as:

- Building skills and confidence in communication, such as writing or speaking
- Branching out socially and engaging with new people
- Cultivating healthy ways to deal with confusion and anxiety (stress-reduction)
- Making time for stimulating activities, such as taking a class, learning a craft or joining a discussion group
- Stepping out of tendencies to over-think emotions
- Exploring media, journalism, and other information flows
- Embarking on successful commercial activities
- Releasing tendencies to assume another's point of view
- Replacing certainty with curiosity
- Breaking the habit to overachieve
- Healing for lungs and nervous system

Cancer

New Moon Invocation
Inviting Support

Occurs each year when the Sun is in Cancer
(June 21 - July 22)

Cancer is the sign of the Crab and is sensitive, emotional and nurturing. It is ruled by the Moon, and as such is changeable and goes through light and dark phases. Using the energy of this New Moon we call in the power to take responsibility for our own feelings and to help others feel more comfortable with their own emotional states.

With Cancer, we have an opportunity to tune into the archetypal Feminine, finding ways to balance periods of activity with time for deep reflection and inner work.

Cancer is also associated with the imagination and the need to break out of shells in order to grow. Some crabs do this several times in the course of one life cycle. At certain points, they begin to outgrow their shells and start growing a new shell underneath the old one. When the new one cracks through the surface, the old outer covering is shed. For a while the crab will be more vulnerable to attack, as the new shell is not as hard as the old one yet.

With the New Moon in Cancer, we are encouraged to dip into the waters of our own vulnerability and to imagine the ways we can share our emotions with others. In order to do this, we need to acknowledge the people, places and things that make us feel safe enough to show up. Learning to be in alignment with Cancer is learning how to be safe while simultaneously remaining sensitive and alive to new feelings and experiences of growth.

So what is it that makes you feel emotionally secure and loved? With Cancer, we have to deal with experiences from the past that have created deeper issues and problems in our current lives. This is a good time to own up to what needs to be resolved, healed and/or released. Are there places you have been holding on to your emotions? Where would you like to cultivate more nurturing toward yourself and others?

Specific intentions for this New Moon can focus on areas ruled by Cancer, such as:

- Inviting time for personal reflection into your daily life
- Practicing self-care
- Creating a supportive home for yourself
- Learning how to offer support to others without violating boundaries
- Restoring a healthy relationship with food
- Nurturing your body
- Spending more time with your family
- Stepping out of tendencies to overreact to emotions
- Letting go of defensive armor
- Healing old wounds, especially in regard to mothers and relationships with women in general
- Honoring the power of vulnerability
- Healing for breasts and stomach

Leo

♌

New Moon Invocation
Heart's Desire

Occurs each year when the Sun is in Leo
(July 23 - August 22)

Leo is the sign of the Lion: proud, dramatic and playful. It is ruled by the Sun, and so signifies the radiant energy of life that shines its warmth down on the Earth. The Sun is our will and our fire; it is what we came here to do.

Using the energy of this New Moon we can set intentions to direct our efforts into areas that empower and revitalize rather than drain our energy. If there are activities that create a spirit of enthusiasm within you, the Leo New Moon invites you to participate.

Leo rules the heart, getting us in touch with our heart's desire, that which we long to create and actualize in our lives. If we are blocking our natural inner radiance, this New Moon is a good time to ask for help in removing these blocks.

With Leo, we have the chance to open to the child within and move more playfully and gracefully through challenging circumstances. Take time this New Moon to ask yourself where you would like to activate the energy of playfulness and joy in your life. Get in touch with your heart's desire, whether it's the passion to create or the passion to relate, and set intentions that help you take the step forward to manifesting that desire.

When the Moon is in Leo, we can take a look at the talents and abilities hidden within us that are begging to be acknowledged. Are there areas in which you'd like to develop your leadership abilities? Do you ever let your pride stop you from giving/receiving love?

Specific intentions for this New Moon can focus on areas ruled by Leo, such as:

- Cultivating more drama, glamour or courage in your life
- Entering a new romance or rekindling the romance in your current relationship
- Opening more to love
- Giving and receiving more healthy attention from loved ones
- Releasing feelings of superiority or inferiority that block you from the love of others and self
- Embarking on a new creative path or art project
- Inviting time for self-love and appreciation into your life
- Invoking the spirit of generosity in your daily activities
- Stepping into leadership roles
- Creating healthy relationships with children or your own inner child
- Bringing a sense of playfulness to life
- Healing for heart, upper back and spine

Virgo

♍

New Moon Invocation
Simplify your Life

Occurs each year when the Sun is in Virgo
(August 23 - September 22)

Virgo is the sign of the Virgin and symbolizes sovereignty. To be sovereign means that one is accorded one's rightful status, independence or prerogative. Through Virgo we are able to discover our birthright, fully embodying the person we came here to be.

Virgo helps us get clear about what we really need and what's outlived its purpose. With its discerning, judging mind, Virgo cuts away the threads of distraction to make order out of chaos.

Use this New Moon to call in the energy of simplicity, to create living conditions and work spaces that are in touch with your personal preferences and inner needs. Virgo is the sign of the Servant and Priestess, which means using our talents and skills to serve others in meaningful ways.

The New Moon in Virgo can help us set intentions in the areas of health and nutrition. Perhaps we aren't recognizing what our bodies need to stay fit and can use this time to ask for support from healthcare providers. Virgo Moons like helping us create rituals that bring the sacred into the every day. How one bathes, cooks, eats and other daily necessities can be a source of inspiration and connection if they are imbued with meaning.

Take some time to think about your own skills and abilities. Paring down your focus to just one or two can help you see with greater clarity the tools you are here to utilize in service to others.

As the sky grows dark with the New Moon energy, ask yourself if there are areas of your life that feel too cluttered or are lacking in focus. Does your inner perfectionist stop you from doing things that you love? How do you serve others?

Specific intentions for this New Moon can focus on areas ruled by Virgo, such as:

- Finding the right job or creating healthy work habits
- Invoking the spirit of discernment in order to make clear decisions
- Releasing the need to be perfect
- Letting go of tendencies to worry, criticize or judge self/others
- Reducing clutter and inviting more order and efficiency into your life
- Focusing on the body-mind connection, through yoga or other physical-spiritual practices
- Freeing yourself from the habit of overworking or overextending yourself
- Learning more about health, healing and nutrition
- Spending time alone
- Cultivating humility, grounded-ness and acceptance of what is
- Making order out of chaos
- Healing for digestive system, especially the intestines

Libra

♎

New Moon Invocation
Balancing Act

Occurs each year when the Sun is in Libra
(September 23 - October 22)

Libra is the sign of the scales and symbolizes our human desire for balance and just outcomes. Libra is sensitive to others, charming and social by nature. Libra is ruled by Venus, goddess of relating, and can assist us in developing good social graces.

Use the power of this New Moon to call in what you need to restore balance and beauty to your life. It could be that your home is crying out for a do-over. Libra can help with that. Or maybe it's your love-life that needs revamping. Libra's here to lend a hand. If you want to see yourself in a more flattering light, the Libra Moon can put things in perspective.

Libra wants to create peace where there is discord and bring more beauty and grace into our world. Libra's world is not free of tension, but teaches us how to navigate conflict in order to cultivate win-win situations in which everyone flourishes. Rather than repressing the imbalance, look within for hidden motivations, conditions, or judgments whenever strife arises. When we are avoiding our inner work, sometimes the Powers That Be will swoop in to get our attention through the actions of (annoying) people in our lives. If there are people or situations that are really getting to you, check yourself first.

Working with Venus, the goddess of love, we can create a sense of luxury, beautify our homes and smooth out difficult relationships. What is beautiful to you? Are there tendencies or roles you play in relationships that you would like to release? Do you struggle with co-dependency or a fear of commitment? Are you satisfied with the quality of your social life?

Specific intentions for this New Moon can focus on areas ruled by Libra, such as:

- Embarking on home- or self-beautification projects
- Finding resolution for interpersonal conflicts
- Seeing yourself and others accurately, without bias or projection
- Finding freedom from indecision
- Healing from mental exhaustion
- Collaborating with others
- Extending yourself socially, making new friends
- Receiving and opening to more beauty, luxury and grace
- Giving and receiving support in mutually beneficial partnerships
- Invoking diplomacy, compromise and cooperation in relationships
- Releasing tendencies to withhold your point of view
- Learning how to speak your truth
- Healing for kidneys or adrenal system

Scorpio
♏

New Moon Invocation
Entering the Darkness

Occurs each year when the Sun is in Scorpio
(October 23 - November 21)

Scorpio is the sign of the Scorpion and the Eagle, and is co-ruled by the planets Mars and Pluto. With Scorpio we can soar to heights of power and perspective, and we can dive deep below the surface to understand the darkness. When the Moon is in Scorpio, emotions are definitely intense, arising from unconscious desires.

Use the power of this New Moon to call in emotional security and self-mastery. Support may come from a spiritual path, a therapist's couch, or an understanding friend. Scorpio wants us to uncover our own darkness. In so doing, we may find the courage and strength to transform our lives and the capacity to open to others more deeply than we thought possible.

The mythic figure of the phoenix reminds us of the power within Scorpio. This magical bird sings a song only he can sing before falling to the earth in flames. After a time, he rises again from the ashes, reborn.

What do you feel about death? How are you resistant or addicted to change? What are the gifts of darkness? What part of your life is ready to be transformed?

Specific intentions for this New Moon can focus on areas ruled by Scorpio, such as:

- Healing past abuse, betrayal or other trauma
- Calling in support for personal growth and transformation
- Releasing suspicion, jealousy and shame in relationships
- Understanding tendencies to create crisis
- Reducing risks to personal safety
- Finding healthy expressions of power in relationships
- Finding one's soul-mate
- Honoring sexuality
- Working to secure loans or eliminating debt for financial success
- Investigating issues of grief, death and dying
- Beginning a process of self-exploration through therapy or other psychological support
- Healing for male and female sexual organs
- Healing for the organs of elimination (bladder, rectum, colon, etc.)

Sagittarius

New Moon Invocation
Faith

Occurs each year when the Sun is in Sagittarius
(November 22 - December 21)

Sagittarius is a fire sign symbolized by the Archer and the Centaur. It is ruled by the planet Jupiter. This planet and sign energy can be associated with the *Fortune* and *Temperance* cards in the Tarot. Both cards encourage us to find the center of things, so that we take the highs and lows of life in stride. With this New Moon, we may find ourselves looking for a faith path, belief system, or other meaningful order to help us do just that.

Sagittarius is looking for the meaning behind human enterprises so that we can build worlds capable of holding these greater truths. This meaning can be held by philosophy, intellectual exploration, cultural expression or spiritual faith. Sagittarius seeks to expand our horizons even as we come to know the center of things more intimately.

When the Moon is in Sagittarius, we can feel more optimistic and outgoing. Conversely, we may feel drawn to the quieter side of Sagittarius, symbolized by the guru who withdraws from the material world in order to gain insight into the higher realms of consciousness. Sagittarius can impart exuberance and social gaiety, but it's also wise to look for ways to inhabit your authentic self with this New Moon while tending to any holiday obligations. Take time to reflect on what's truly important to you. Find the center in the great turning wheel of your life.

What do you need to renew your faith in life, self or spirit? What does abundance mean to you? Do you have a sense of your Higher Self, your spiritual purpose?

Specific intentions for this New Moon can focus on areas ruled by Sagittarius, such as:

- Connecting to your intuition and your Higher Self
- Calling in the spirit of adventure
- Releasing cynicism and pessimistic tendencies
- Furthering your education or embarking on a new path of study
- Eliminating waste or excess (e.g. eating, drinking, spending)
- Beginning a new spiritual or philosophical practice, such as meditation or divination
- Calling in the energy of abundance
- Finding your core – what sustains you through life's ups and downs
- Resolving legal matters
- Embarking on foreign travel or the study of languages
- Taking chances that are right for your life
- Healing for hips, thighs and liver

Capricorn

♑

New Moon Invocation
Integrity

Occurs each year when the Sun is in Capricorn
(December 22 - January 19)

Capricorn is an earth sign, symbolized by the goat, an animal that can scale the highest peaks of impossibly steep mountains. It is often associated with the qualities of discipline, responsibility and authority. The deeper meaning of Capricorn is to find balance between inner and outer reality.

When we are out of alignment with ourselves, we will eventually slip and fall. Keeping a stiff upper lip may help us push through to the end, but at some point we will have to pay the costs of denying an inner state or an outer condition that could use some more structure or discipline. Examples of this are ignoring the concerns of others in order to accomplish something you want, or putting your own needs last for the sake of a group project or goal. In the end, this can deplete us of energy and perhaps lead to feelings of inferiority even when we succeed.

Use the energy of the New Moon to imagine what sort of structures can help build the life you want. Listen to your inner authority and ask yourself if anything needs to be adjusted in order to get you back into alignment with your deeper purpose.

What is your relationship with authority? Are there places in your life where you are too serious or not serious enough? What does it mean to be responsible? What do your emotions have to do with responsibility? What are you here to learn?

Specific intentions for this New Moon can focus on areas ruled by Capricorn, such as:

- Inviting in the spirit of discipline, a commitment to the practice of learning
- Committing to your goals
- Building or repairing your public image
- Invoking mature decision-making processes
- Letting go of self-limiting thoughts and fears
- Cultivating a healthy relationship with time
- Becoming the master of your trade
- Stepping into your authority
- Taking on more or less responsibility at work
- Releasing the need to "do it all"
- Balancing home life with work life
- Making decisions about your career and professional life
- Healing for bones, joints and teeth

Aquarius

♒

New Moon Invocation
Awakening the Inner Genius
Occurs each year when the Sun is in Aquarius
(January 20 - February 18)

Airy Aquarius is the sign of freedom, individuality and the spark of genius that lives in each of us. Co-ruled by Saturn and Uranus, Aquarius needs to be "in the flow" of time, ideas and social interactions so that it can bring its uniqueness and innovation to the world.

Timing is everything with Aquarius. It rules such topics as our hopes and fears, our visions, our connections with others, and our recognition of patterns. Which things manifest (or not) in our lives often depends upon how events unfold and whether (or not) we notice that the right time has come to take action. This energy also encourages us to see how others can help us realize our dreams.

Use the New Moon in Aquarius to tap into your own inner genius, the part of you that may be a bit odd and eccentric but holds a vital piece of our collective puzzle. Recently, some astrologers have likened Aquarius' co-ruler Uranus with the Greek figure of Prometheus who stole fire from the gods and gave it to the humans. With this selfless act, he made civilization and culture possible. We can listen to this part of ourselves whenever we need to shake things up in order to make positive changes for ourselves and the world.

How are you like Prometheus? Where do you need this spirit of change in your life to break down the old order? Do you feel like an outsider or different from those around you? How is this a strength and/or challenge?

Specific intentions for this New Moon can focus on areas ruled by Aquarius, such as:

- Looking to the future and opening to your visionary self
- Creating healthy friendships and broadening community networks
- Finding creative and surprising solutions to long-standing problems
- Working with time in new ways and noticing synchronicity
- Letting go of emotional detachment
- Seeing the Big Picture and letting go of the small stuff
- Considering the needs of others and humanitarian goals in decision-making
- Liberating yourself from deadening or restrictive structures
- Feeding your wildest hopes and dreams
- Embracing your inner freak
- Releasing tendencies to distance yourself from others
- Healing for nervous system, circulation , ankles and calves

Pisces

New Moon Invocation
Unity

Occurs each year when the Sun is in Pisces
(February 19 - March 20)

Co-ruled by Jupiter and Neptune, watery Pisces is often called the sign of mysticism and spirituality. While its underlying message of unity and cosmic belonging can be found in experiences of spirit, we enter the realm of Pisces whenever we find an opportunity to transcend our individual labels and suffering. Pisces needs dreams, music and faith; it prefers poetry and feelings over facts.

The energy of this New Moon can bring idealism and profound vision to an area of our lives that has been weighted down by negativity or cynicism. It can also help us understand our individual suffering from a broader viewpoint. This moon wants us to cultivate compassion for ourselves and others in order to identify with an underlying unity of life. Listen to this part of you in order to release attachments to illusion and to dream new dreams.

Where do you need more reverie and imagination in your life? What are the ways that Spirit speaks to you? Where are you currently experiencing suffering?

To tap into the energy of this New Moon, you can create a ritual of writing out your intentions and burning them with herbs as offerings or hanging them on a wall as a reminder throughout the next lunar cycle.

Specific intentions for this New Moon can focus on areas ruled by Pisces, such as:

- Healing for addictions
- Finding forgiveness for past wounds
- Releasing tendencies to take on the role of the victim/martyr in relationships
- Releasing negative thinking
- Beginning or deepening one's spiritual practice, such as meditation, ritual or dream work
- Inviting in a fresh relationship with the Divine, finding new spiritual awareness
- Developing acceptance and compassion for self and others
- Creating time for stress relief, quiet reflection and "down time"
- Activating the imagination, dreams, healing talents and psychic abilities
- Shedding self-delusion, confusion and damaging fantasies about self and others
- Making time for imaginative exploration in art, music, poetry, film and dance
- Healing for feet, lymphatic system or sleep disorders

The Power of the Full Moon

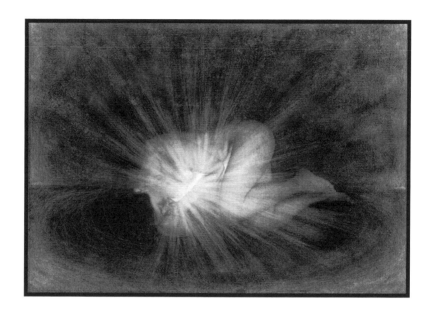

"Listen to the words of the Great Mother, Who of old was called Artemis, Astarte, Dione, Melusine, Aphrodite, Cerridwen, Diana, Arionrhod, Brigid, and by many other names:

"Whenever you have need of anything, once a month, and better it be when the moon is full, you shall assemble in some secret place and adore the spirit of Me Who is Queen of all the Wise."

~ from *The Charge of the Goddess* by Doreen Valiente

With the New Moon, we set intentions and planted seeds for the future. As the Moon grows over the days and weeks, so too our wishes and projects may flourish and reach a point of culmination. Although many intentions take years or even a lifetime to fulfill, the Full Moon shining brilliantly down at us each month reminds us of the possibility of reaching such wholeness.

The Full Moon carries the energy of culmination and celebration. Projects completed, accomplishments noted, recognition received, harvests collected: the full moon can bring all of these things and more.

But the energy of the Full Moon is not always joyous. The Moon symbolizes our emotional state, our inner knowing, and our physical wellness. If we have been bottling anything up – repressing, ignoring or dismissing what we feel – then the Full Moon will certainly take those feelings and unleash them. Consider the werewolf, who is a normal human being for 25 days but becomes a wild beast for the three nights when the Moon is in its fullness. Just like the werewolf, we may go a bit crazy when the Moon comes into peak intensity. The words *lunacy* and *lunatic* come directly from the Latin word for moon: *luna*. Incidences of wild behavior, increases of crime and an overall air of intensity is said to correspond to a Full Moon.

Whenever the Moon is full, we can align with this energy by gathering together with others in celebration and joy. We can reserve this time for cutting loose and going a bit wild. This can release tension and blocks in our lives.

Indeed, Full Moon magic is all about release. Like the fruit hanging low on the vines, ready for harvest, or the baby carried to full term now ready for birth, the Full Moon says, "Now is the time!"

Full Moons can also help us release negative emotions or dispel unhealthy energy in general. Whether in a relationship, in your home or other areas of life, we may see more clearly the things that aren't working and make room for change.

Taken altogether, it's intense. Whenever the Moon is full, we tend to have big feelings and these feelings come out in all kinds of unpredictable ways. Fights happen. Outbursts burst out. The tempo speeds up. We just can't take it anymore!

When we know that the Full Moon is coming, we can adjust ourselves accordingly. Sometimes just knowing that the energy is building is enough. We don't have to *do* anything about it. Other times, the build-up is telling us that it's time to release something, whether in a celebration or a grand purging.

As British singer Seal tells us, "we're never, ever gonna survive unless we get a little crazy." The Full Moon gives us permission to do just that each month. Making room in your life for some Full Moon magic might make the lunacy a little less destructive.

Full Moons amplify the energy of a sign. Each Full Moon is in opposition to the Sun, which means that the solar energy of a specific time – what we are focusing *conscious will* on - will be challenged by the energy of the moon – what we need on the mysterious soul level.

In the following pages, we'll take a look at the Full Moon in each sign in order to understand the themes that might pop up unannounced at your emotional door each month. You may want to begin tracking the Full Moon each month, noticing what you experience and feel and jotting down a few words to describe it. In this way, you'll begin to build a map of your own lunar consciousness and discover ways that help you stay balanced and whole even when the energy of your life surges in unexpected directions. Again, the month in which you can expect each Full Moon in a certain sign is given, although the precise dates will vary from year to year.

Because Full Moons are about creative fruition and lighting up the current energy, I find that building altars can be a powerful, fun and easy way to participate with this lunar phase. How do you build an altar – and what is an altar anyway? Let's find out:

altar - *noun*

1. an elevated place or structure, as a mound or platform, at which religious rites are performed or on which sacrifices are offered to gods, ancestors, etc.

The word altar has its origins in the Latin *adolare* meaning "burnt offerings" and *altus* meaning "high." Elevating the place that offerings are given reveals an altar's purpose: to move our human consciousness higher so that it may commune with the forces of spirit.

I am interested in how the words altar and alter are homonyms – words that are spelled differently but sound alike. These two words seem to have connected meanings as well. To build an *altar* is to attempt to consciously *alter* an outcome. In the old days, I might burn or kill something in order to appease some god and make him look upon me beneficently. In this case, I am using an *altar* to offer a sacrifice and thereby *alter* my relationship with a god.

Today, we don't have to kill anything or even sacrifice much in order to utilize altars as a tool for deepening our connection with the Divine. Altars can be built anywhere – on a bedside table, in the crook of a tree, on dashboards, or in a special place in your home. Altars are spaces that we have intentionally set aside to honor, worship and connect with what is holy or important to us. An altar is a place to set out objects that symbolize something we value and hold in high esteem. This is why they are a particularly good form of Full Moon magic. At the height of the Moon's light and power, we may want to honor our own light and power; we may want to say thanks for something we have received; we may want to create a place to help ourselves ground in times of intensity. An altar can help us do that.

To build an altar, you don't need any fancy-shmancy objects. You don't need to go out and buy anything. The things you can find around your home or out in the natural world will do just fine. Choose where you would like to build your altar. A table cloth or other pretty fabric can cover a table or serve as the base for your altar even without a table. Next, simply take some time to reflect and sink into the energy of why you'd like to build this particular altar. Some reasons might be to express gratitude for a relationship, to celebrate a recent accomplishment, or to amplify the energy of some area in your life. Once you feel clear about the purpose, then you wander. Just wander around the house, yard, neighborhood or nearby park. Gather things that you feel have a resonance with your mission. When you have some objects gathered, you can begin to assemble them on your altar. Make it pretty, intriguing or satisfying to your eyes and heart. When you're done, spend some time with it. Let the Full Moon charge it with its specific energy. Leave your altar up as long as it feels alive to you. When the energy seems to have drained or waned – just like our fair Moon in the sky – take it down, treating each object respectfully.

I love building altars. They are these delicious temporary pieces of art that contain a beautiful purpose. I don't always have one up in my house, but usually I do. Sometimes I am creating new altars every week and sometimes I go for a whole season with the same one. It depends on the altar and what its purpose is.

At the end of each section, you will find ideas and inspirations for altar building on the Full Moon. There are suggestions for themes, colors, certain plants and herbs* that are related to the astrological sign of the Full Moon. All the ideas offered here are merely a starting point for your own investigation. As you venture out into your own imagination and world to see what needs to be honored, thanked, celebrated or released, you may find other ways of marking the Full Moon. There's space given for you to record your own notes, feelings and observations.

Altars are good to build for New Moon intentions as well, but the Full Moon each month is so showy, I think it deserves a visible representation to shine down on. The Full Moon can charge, or amplify, a particular energy. It can remind us to be grateful for what we have. It can banish the darkness and release us from inner-prisons. Full Moon altars are a great way to honor the sacred in your life, putting what is dear and lovely to you in a high place, so that the light can reach it.

*Please note: plant and herb suggestions should not be taken as medical advice. The plants listed are generally in bloom or seasonal according to the time of the Full Moon, and the herbs are related to the specific physical system ruled over by the astrological sign.

Libra

♎

Full Moon Spotlight
Facing the Other
Occurs each year when the Sun is in Aries
(March 21 - April 19)

With the Full Moon in Libra, the focus is on the mysterious "other." In the circle of the Zodiac, Libra is the point of balance, bringing us face to face with opposing forces. These "others" can look like partners, friends, enemies or even our own inner conflicts. When we feel at odds in our relationships, Libra reminds us to look in the mirror first before blaming others.

Libra is the sign of partnership and collaboration. When we are honest about our own needs and desires, Libra can show us the way to cooperate and find power through linking with other people.

For this Full Moon, you may feel the call to partner up with others in order to manifest your desires, or you may feel the challenge of compromise. Look for the ways that you foster harmony and balance in your life. Celebrate your own creativity, beauty and humor, and take the time to appreciate the traits you admire in others.

Tell people what you like about them. Let go of the need to be in charge all the time. Although a Full Moon in Libra can intensify the conflict within relationships right now, working with others ultimately might be the way to get exactly what you need.

- How do you deal with conflict?
- What are your favorite things to collaborate on?
- Who are the people in your "inner-circle" of friends?
- How do you show and receive love from others?
- What is beautiful to you?

Themes for your Full Moon in Libra Altar
Relationships, Balancing of Needs, Beauty, Truth-telling

Planetary Ruler
Venus

Element
Air: Thinking

Mode
Cardinal: Initiating

Gender
Masculine: Active

Colors
Scarlet, White

Gemstones
Coral, Diamond, Copper

Seasonal Plants
Daffodils, Rosemary

Herbal Friends
Nettles, Cleavers (Good for the Kidneys)

Notes, feelings and observations for the Full Moon in Libra:

Scorpio

♏

Full Moon Spotlight
Mystery and Transformation

Occurs each year when the Sun is in Taurus
(April 20 - May 20)

With the Full Moon in Scorpio, the focus is on journeying into the intense fires of change in order to discover true intimacy and personal power. Scorpio desires union, two things coming together to make something new, but it is also a sign of separation and death. What it is searching for in both union and separation is the essence or energy that operates underneath our conscious striving.

The polarity of Scorpio is Taurus, the sign of stability, sensual pleasure and the material world. With Scorpio, we seek to dip below the surface of the material world in order to find connection that transcends the personal. The dark side of Scorpio can work on us through intense emotional drama that seems to erupt from nowhere. For this Full Moon, you may be forced to confront your own jealousy, possessiveness or emotional manipulation.

Tension can run high in relationships, and you may feel overly sensitive to other people's words and energies. But it is most likely our subconscious desires that are calling the shots. Take an honest look at your own feelings and needs. When the time is right, find an honest and open way to work with those issues. True intimacy and inner transformation go hand in hand when we are willing to discuss our needs and listen with openness to the needs of our loved ones.

This is a moon to celebrate your own magical power and to engage in divination or other spiritual tools that align you with the unseen forces that guide you.

- How do you honor your passion and intensity?
- What is your relationship with darkness, uncertainty and mystery?
- In what ways are you strong and resilient?

Themes for your Full Moon in Scorpio Altar
Releasing, Elimination, Transformation, Purification

Planetary Ruler
Mars, Pluto

Element
Water: Feeling

Mode
Fixed: Stabilizing

Gender
Feminine: Receptive

Colors
Indigo, Dark Shades

Gemstones
Smoky Quartz, Bloodstone

Seasonal Plants
Dogwoods, Lilac, Azalea

Herbal Friends
Yellow Dock, Cascara Sagrada (Good for the Organs of Elimination)

Notes, feelings and observations for the Full Moon in Scorpio:

Sagittarius

Full Moon Spotlight
Meaningful Growth
Occurs each year when the Sun is in Gemini
(May 21 - June 20)

With the Full Moon in Sagittarius, the focus is on expanding our boundaries and engaging in growth that is meaningful and increases our faith in life. Sagittarius is on a quest for truth and wisdom. The symbol for Sagittarius is the archer shooting his arrow into the future with an adventurous optimism.

It is also pictured as the centaur, half-horse and half-human, grounded in the earthly plane yet reaching for the stars. Animal and human at once, the centaur has instinctual power as well as intellectual potential. The animal is full of passion, while the human seeks to translate experience into broader expressions of truth. No wonder that teachers, philosophers and culture-makers are associated with this sign.

We may feel the urge to travel or break away from constraints during this time. This is a friendly and optimistic Moon, looking for the next adventure. But its shadow shows a propensity to over-commit and a need to stretch the truth to suit our own purposes.

This Full Moon reminds us that getting in touch with our Higher Self is essential to living a life of purpose and joy.

This week, you may feel like joining in with others to gain different perspectives, or you may crave some personal space. Clear away the distractions of the material world, reconnect with nature or leap into a new experience that stretches you out of your normal ways of seeing.

- Are there areas of life in which you are blinded by faith or overly skeptical?
- Is it time for a wild adventure or some quiet time?
- What ways do you enjoy new experiences?
- Do you act from a place of faith or a place of fear?

Themes for your Full Moon in Sagittarius Altar
Growth, Spiritual Meaning, Abundance

Planetary Ruler
Jupiter

Element
Fire: Intuitive

Mode
Mutable: Adapting

Gender
Masculine: Active

Colors
Purple, Blue

Gemstones
Yellow Sapphire, Topaz

Seasonal Plants
Birch, Columbine

Herbal Friends
Milk Thistle, Dandelion, Oregon Grape (Tonics for the Liver)

Notes, feelings and observations for the Full Moon in Sagittarius:

Capricorn
♑

Full Moon Spotlight
Time for a Reality Check
Occurs each year when the Sun is in Cancer
(June 21 - July 22)

With the Full Moon in Capricorn, the focus is on hard work and responsibility. Capricorn is often viewed as a more practical and less emotional sign, so with this Full Moon we can expect a certain amount of conflict between these two spheres, as well as between our personal and public lives. Trying to "keep it together" may be very difficult during this phase, and we may want to run away from some commitments.

There is also a danger of being insensitive to our own or others' feelings, preferring to focus on the practical side of things. But shutting information out will not necessarily keep us on track.

What this Full Moon wants is for us to recognize our limitations and to keep focusing on the present moment in order to complete the task at hand. We will do well to honor our obligations while staying grounded in what is realistically possible given our present circumstances. If we try to do too much, we could easily fall into a gloom-and-doom outlook and infect our own hearts and relationships with a lot of unnecessary negative energy.

This Full Moon reminds us that true responsibility is sustainable; it comes from seeking structures that support both our individual needs and our broader relationships.

- Are there places where you are too hard on yourself?
- Are you limiting your own potential by staying trapped in negative thinking or by blocking certain types of thoughts or feelings?
- Where would you like to have more industriousness and discipline in your life?
- How could you turn your shortcomings into assets?

Themes for your Full Moon in Capricorn Altar
Discipline, Responsibility, Status

Planetary Ruler
Saturn

Element
Earth: Sensing

Mode
Cardinal: Initiating

Gender
Feminine: Receptive

Colors
Black, blue-violet

Gemstones
Onyx, Jet, Turquoise

Seasonal Plants
Rose, Lavender, Calendula

Herbal Friends
Comfrey, Horsetail (Good for Bone Health)

Notes, feelings and observations for the Full Moon in Capricorn:

Aquarius

♒

Full Moon Spotlight
The Big Picture

Occurs each year when the Sun is in Leo
(July 23 - August 22)

With the Full Moon in Aquarius, the focus is on freedom, intellectual exchange and humanitarianism. We may feel friendlier toward others and quicker to offer help out of a desire for mutual liberation. This is generally a less emotionally driven, more rational Full Moon, as we strive to put emotional reactions aside and work out our problems intellectually for the overall welfare of society. The energy of the Aquarian Full Moon asks us to honor our own uniqueness as it relates to building more humane groups and better ways of organizing.

Aquarius is co-ruled by the planets Saturn, the stern task-master, and Uranus, the awakener, so the power of this Full Moon is definitely intense. We see the limits and feel the pressure to engage, while also experiencing breakdowns and breakthroughs in consciousness. We may feel flooded with uplifting ideas and energy at this time or feel fizzle-fried and isolated by the frenetic pace of our lives. Our minds can create brilliant visions of the future or spin us into high anxiety and fear. Instead of fearing the future, we can take time to celebrate the communities we belong to and to revel in our unique gifts.

We have the chance here to see the big picture and to see how our individuality plays an important role in the shaping of the collective. It may be time to shift some focus from the "I" to a bigger, more powerful "We."

- Are there ways you let your specialness marginalize you from others?
- Are you afraid of rocking the boat?
- What are your hopes and fears for the future?

Themes for your Full Moon in Aquarius Altar
Community, The Future, Innovation, Uniqueness

Planetary Ruler
Saturn, Uranus

Element
Air: Thinking

Mode
Fixed: Stabilizing

Gender
Masculine: Active

Colors
Electric Blue, Multi-hued colors

Gemstones
Sapphire, Opal

Seasonal Plants
Borage, Hydrangea,
Delphinium

Herbal Friends
Ginger, Cayenne (Good for Circulation)

Notes, feelings and observations for the Full Moon in Aquarius:

Pisces

Full Moon Spotlight
Compassion

Occurs each year when the Sun is in Virgo
(August 23 - September 22)

When the Full Moon in Pisces lights up the sky, focus on building your sense of compassion and creating some down time for yourself. You may find this to be a good time to reawaken your connections to spirit and find direction for your soul's path.

This Full Moon has everyone feeling more sensitive than usual, so be mindful of how you interact with loved ones. You may feel more vulnerable, confused and impressionable, and the desire to retreat will be strong. We could really feel the weight of the world with this Full Moon, drawing attention to our own short-comings, suffering and illusions of life. It's a good time to reflect on such themes, but be careful not to get lost in the deep end. Retreat is a good thing, but isolation can also heighten our painful feelings. Be especially mindful of using alcohol, drugs or other methods of escaping your problems.

To harness the energy in positive ways, engage in activities that are restorative and healing, such as being in water, meditating or listening to soothing music. If we look to ourselves and the world through the lens of Piscean compassion, we can release long-standing patterns of suffering, such as the victim-martyr conditioning in relationships.

Use this moon to deepen your intuitive capabilities by focusing on dreams, visions and other spiritual channels.

- Where do you find inspiration and emotional sustenance?
- How do you reconnect with the Divine?
- What are the ways you bring healing to the world?

Themes for your Full Moon in Pisces Altar
Unity, Compassion, Spiritual Awareness

Planetary Ruler
Jupiter, Neptune

Element
Water: Feeling

Mode
Mutable: Adapting

Gender
Feminine: Receptive

Colors
Violet, Rainbow

Gemstones
Amethyst, Aquamarine

Seasonal Plants
Mugwort, Dahlia, Echinacea

Herbal Friends
Cleavers, Red Root (Good for the Lymphatic System)

Notes, feelings and observations for the Full Moon in Pisces:

Aries

♈

Full Moon Spotlight
Honoring the Impulse
Occurs each year when the Sun is in Libra
(September 23 - October 22)

With the Full Moon in Aries, the focus is on our individualism and pioneering spirit. Aries is the first sign of the zodiac and wants to be first in everything. The symbol of Aries is the ram, an animal that plunges headfirst into confrontation.

The days before and after a Full Moon are very emotionally charged, and with Aries we can expect intense passion and power to fuel our actions and encounters with others. What this Full Moon wants is for you to honor the impulse and empower your life without burning bridges, burning out or burning up in anger.

With Aries, we have to find mature outlets for our power and passion, such as competitive sports or activities where there is the potential for risk. It's a good time to examine the inner warrior, that part of us that wants to take actions to protect or create boundaries. We may leap to defend a cause, idea or person we care about. If we are failing to heed our own impulses, we can expect them to come out as anger, frustration and tantrums directed at anyone in our path.

Instead of adolescent outbursts, strive to listen to your inner warrior and see what s/he needs to feel empowered. Call in the pioneering spirit of this Aries Full Moon to navigate uncharted emotional terrain.

This Full Moon ushers us into the introspective time of year by forcing us to look deeply at our emotional wellbeing, our desires and our unexpressed individual needs.

- Have you been letting others take advantage of you?
- Are there projects that have been in the dreaming stage for too long?
- What have harvested from previous actions in the past year?

Themes for your Full Moon in Aries Altar
Individuality, Strength, Sexuality, Courage

Planetary Ruler
Mars

Element
Fire: Intuitive

Mode
Cardinal: Initiating

Gender
Masculine: Active

Colors
Reds, burnt orange

Gemstones
Carnelian, Tiger's eye

Seasonal Plants
Sunflowers, Anemone, Cosmos

Herbal Friends
Skullcap, Valerian, Hops (Good for reducing stress and tension)

Notes, feelings and observations for the Full Moon in Aries:

Taurus

♉

Full Moon Spotlight
Celebrating the Senses

Occurs each year when the Sun is in Scorpio
(October 23 - November 21)

With the Full Moon in Taurus, the focus is on sensual pleasure and practical preparation. Taurus, ruled by the planet Venus, is an earth sign symbolized by the Bull. While it is primarily focused on the personal side of the earth element, namely personal safety and security, it is also a symbol of the luscious, abundant Earth itself. When the Moon is in Taurus, personal issues around possessions and material security are indeed pushed to the surface. At this time of year, we may feel the urge to prepare for the coming winter months to ensure survival. It's time to check in with our resources and make sure we are using them wisely. Finish up any lingering projects or check in with your goals for those projects.

To connect to the power of this Full Moon in Taurus, take some time to luxuriate in the senses. Taurus loves indulging in beauty and sensuality, so slow down a bit, get that massage, sit down by that fire and open to the energy of your body.

Focus on what's necessary in your life to find balance with the living systems of Earth, instead of accumulating a protective barrier of "stuff." Trees in autumn know how to shed their leaves and channel their energy to their roots for the winter. Our own survival requires that we change as well as preserve, that we let go of some things even as we gather others. Ask yourself what you have a hard time letting go of. Enjoy what you have, acknowledge your wealth of skills, and take inspiration from the Spirit of Nature, which is constant and yet always changing.

- What part of you in ready to go underground?
- How can you use your energy efficiently?
- What do you truly need to feel secure emotionally and physically?

Themes for your Full Moon in Taurus Altar
Gratitude, Manifesting, Endurance

Planetary Ruler
Venus

Element
Earth: Sensing

Mode
Fixed: Stabilizing

Gender
Feminine: Receptive

Colors
Green, pastels

Gemstones
Emerald, Malachite, Moss Agate

Seasonal Plants
Fruits and vegetables of the harvest

Herbal Friends
Sage, Echinacea (Good for Sore Throats)

Notes, feelings and observations for the Full Moon in Taurus:

Gemini

♊

Full Moon Spotlight
The Energy of Exchange

Occurs each year when the Sun is in Sagittarius
(November 22 - December 21)

With the Full Moon in Gemini, we can feel a bit flighty and scattered. Our minds may wander and our bodies feel restless. Gemini is about exchanges, whether in commerce, communication or ideas.

Gemini is ruled by the planet Mercury, the Messenger God. Mercury is quick, clever and crafty, and uses his skills of communication to get himself into and out of trouble. When the Moon is in Gemini, we may speak too quickly and say things we later regret. However, this is a great time to change the stories that are keeping us trapped. Get out the pen and write down the ideas and questions you have about your life.

At this time of year, we are pulled in two directions: the winter says "slow down and contemplate," but the holidays cry, "So many parties/gifts/obligations, so little time!" The Gemini Full Moon can help us keep a sense of playfulness and curiosity alive during a time that is often stressful and frenzied.

Remembering to enjoy time with friends and family by focusing on energetic sharing (story-telling, listening, making music, playing games) rather than overemphasizing gift giving can re-ignite our love for winter holidays. Use the Gemini Moon to get into your knitting projects or other handicrafts and throw in some light conversation. Open up your curious mind and try to leave heavy decision-making for another day.

- How do you enjoy spending time with friends?
- What is your favorite thing about the holidays? What are your least favorite things?
- What are the crafts you like to do or the ones you enjoyed as a child?

Themes for your Full Moon in Gemini Altar
Connection, Crafts, Exchanges

Planetary Ruler
Mercury

Element
Air: Thinking

Mode
Mutable: Adapting

Gender
Masculine: Active

Colors
White, yellow, light green

Gemstones
Quartz Crystal

Seasonal Plants
Enjoy fall colors of Maple, Cherry, Gingko

Herbal Friends
Mullein, Thyme (Good for the Lungs)

Notes, feelings and observations for the Full Moon in Gemini:

Cancer

Full Moon Spotlight
The Spotlight Within

Occurs each year when the Sun is in Capricorn
(December 22 - January 19)

With the Full Moon in Cancer, the focus is on the inner landscape of emotions. Cancer is ruled by the Moon and beckons us to our hearts. Cancer's symbol, the Crab, may be covered with a hard shell to protect its soft flesh within, but its purpose is to love and trust without fear. Cancer does need its barriers, but it also has to be willing to open its defenses. Only by connecting with our hearts and sharing these feelings with others, can we grow into fullness.

During this Full Moon, the call is to be responsive to your feelings. You may feel more sentimental and moody. Remember this when you or loved ones get overly nostalgic or fly off the handle about some small irritation. Don't ignore how you feel, but don't let yourself get carried away by these feelings either. Giving yourself the time to look within will help you balance all the responsibilities of your life.

This is a good time to take a look at how your home life is functioning.

- Are you giving yourself time to rest and nourish your body and soul?
- What changes might you make to your living arrangements in order to create a more nurturing home life?
- How do you show your appreciation for the mysterious cycles of your inner world?
- What is your relationship to your emotions?

<u>Themes for your Full Moon in Cancer Altar</u>
Home, Love of Family, Emotional Health

<u>Planetary Ruler</u>
Moon

<u>Element</u>
Water: Feeling

<u>Mode</u>
Cardinal: Initiating

<u>Gender</u>
Feminine: Receptive

<u>Colors</u>
Silver, orange, irrediscent Shades

<u>Gemstones</u>
Moonstone, Abalone

<u>Seasonal Plants</u>
Holly, Camellia, Cedar

<u>Herbal Friends</u>
Marshmallow, Slippery Elm (Good for Stomach)

Notes, feelings and observations for the Full Moon in Cancer:

Leo

♌

Full Moon Spotlight
Drama

Occurs each year when the Sun is in Aquarius
(January 20 - February 18)

With the Full Moon in Leo, the focus is on the playful child, the drama queen and the brave leader. Leo's symbol is the Lion, the king of the jungle, and it is ruled by the fiery, powerful Sun. Leo is the part of us that needs recognition and must create something from its inner world in order to feel whole.

At its best, it is noble and loyal, encouraging others to reach for the stars with the power of its warm heart and enthusiasm for life. When afflicted, Leo spans the spectrum between extreme arrogance and neediness. Leo's shadow side does *anything* for love and seeks only to fulfill its own ego-desires.

With the Full Moon in Leo, drama is on the menu. Drama can be cathartic and fun, served up with flair and playfulness. Or it can be intense and emotional, making impossible demands and throwing tantrums. Try to channel this Leo energy *intentionally* into creative outlets, celebrations, performances or romantic encounters.

This Moon can lift our spirits, giving us a dose of sunshine in our cold winter days. Activate your inner child and play around with your life. If you neglect the need for play, you may be headed for solar-flare eruptions in the form of damaging emotional outbursts.

- How do you let your playful side out?
- Do you need to celebrate yourself and have pride in who you are?
- Are you ready to let go of selfishness, melodrama or arrogance?

Themes for your Full Moon in Leo Altar
Creativity, Children, Matters of the Heart

Planetary Ruler
Sun

Element
Fire: Intuitive

Mode
Fixed: Stablizing

Gender
Masculine: Active

Colors
Gold, Yellow

Gemstones
Amber, Topaz

Seasonal Plants
Hellebore, Crocus, Witch Hazel

Herbal Friends
Hawthorn, Motherwort, Garlic (Heart Tonics)

Notes, feelings and observations for the Full Moon in Leo:

Virgo
♍
Full Moon Spotlight
Integration
Occurs each year when the Sun is in Pisces
(February 19 - March 20)

With the Full Moon in Virgo, the focus is on our overall health and wellbeing. Virgo's symbol is the Virgin, the archetype of the Priestess and Healer who projects the energy of sovereignty, self-awareness, and deep wisdom. Virgo seeks to know herself completely, to cut away the superfluous and keep only what's necessary for the task at hand.

At its best, Virgo accepts herself, flaws and all, and seeks to serve others with the skills she possesses. But Virgo also has a dark side which can get stirred up with the intensity of the Full Moon: a judgmental mind that borders on cruel and an addiction to self-improvement that leaves no time for meaningful work. Virgo can be analytical to the point of inaction. It can also give of itself too much, leading to workaholic tendencies and eventual burn-out.

When the Full Moon is in Virgo, we can see some of these themes more clearly in our lives. We may feel the urge to clean house or reduce clutter in our work space. Hurt feelings can rise up at the perceived criticism of others.

Virgo can help us bring integration into our lives, getting projects, problems and relationships in order. This Full Moon may feel like a searchlight exposing any blemish or shortcoming, but it can also light up the details and activities of our lives that need more awareness and appreciation.

- In which areas of life do you need to re-claim sovereignty, to re-establish boundaries?
- What practices could help you become more mindful and less critical of yourself and others?
- What could use some fine-tuning or editing in your life?
- Is it time to release perfectionism and self-judgment?

Themes for your Full Moon in Virgo Altar
Health, Humility, Looking at Details

Planetary Ruler
Mercury

Element
Earth: Sensing

Mode
Mutable: Adapting

Gender
Feminine: Receptive

Colors
Dark, earthy tones

Gemstones
Marble, Agate

Seasonal Plants
Daffodil, Rosemary

Herbal Friends
Chamomile, Mint, Fennel (Good for Digestion)

Notes, feelings and observations for the Full Moon in Virgo:

Eclipses and the Moon:
Portals of Change

Want the change. Be inspired by the flame
where everything shines as it disappears.
The artist, when sketching,
loves nothing so   much
as the curve of the body as it turns away.

What locks itself in sameness has congealed.
Is it safer to be gray and numb?
What turns hard becomes rigid
and is easily shattered.

Pour yourself out like a fountain.
Flow into the knowledge
that what you are seeking
finishes often at the start, and, with ending, begins.

Every happiness is the child of a separation
it did not think it could survive.
And Daphne, becoming a laurel,
dares you to become the wind.

~ The Sonnets to Orpheus, Part Two, XII
by Rainer Maria Rilke

Eclipses always heighten and intensify our world. They are like super-charged Full and New Moons. With every eclipse season, we have the opportunity to create intentions related to the energy of the signs in which the eclipses are occurring, setting the stage for the coming six months and beyond.

Eclipse cycles happen on the Full and New Moons approximately every six months and act as a kind of energetic bridge through time. We may find ourselves coming to terms with actions we took six months ago, and can even find resolution or illumination about events in our lives from 19 years ago, the last time these specific eclipses would have occurred.

With the Solar Eclipse, which coincides with a New Moon, our intentions are intensified. Ancient Tibetans believed that a New Moon-Solar Eclipse event is "a New Moon times 10,000" in terms of the power available to us for transformation. Along with this, what is different about a Solar Eclipse is that we often receive revelations into some otherwise hidden part of our essential nature. What is literally happening with any Solar Eclipse is that the Moon casts a shadow as it moves across the Sun, obscuring the light. The Moon, our inner nature, is eclipsing the Sun, our conscious desires. We can use the portal created by an eclipse to see into the heart of matters, beyond what our egos may think we need. Here, we are invited (and often pushed) to move by feeling, intuition and hunches instead of exerting our will on the world.

With the Lunar Eclipse, which coincides with the Full Moon, we often recognize new avenues for expression and self-realization. The Lunar Eclipse occurs when the shadow of the Earth blocks the Sun's light. If we've been stuck on the wrong track in our earthly pursuits, the Lunar Eclipse can correct the course. This is not always pleasant. Sometimes, we are pushed off the wrong track and into the mud. We may have to wait a long time there in the muck before we get cleaned up and gain clarity about what happened and why.

But the opportunity here is to begin making our mark on the world in an authentic way instead of settling for a life that isn't really ours. As the energy builds to a Lunar Eclipse, our personal destiny, the part that came here with a clear mission to accomplish – talks things over with our fate and tries to cut some deals. Fate is what can't be changed. However, it can be embraced and utilized as an inner compass that points the way to unfold one's destiny. An eclipse brings about occurrences that force our attention toward correcting any lies we've been telling about ourselves or others. The portal opens, we see the truth, and we make changes in order to let will and destiny make peace with the uncomfortable yet soulfully essential parts of our nature.

Some general advice for the eclipse season is to leave some open space in your schedule. Eclipse periods are full of the unexpected. Projects, people, opportunities and ideas show up suddenly. If you already have a packed calendar, you will definitely get exhausted by the extra attention these surprises require.

Eclipses through the Houses

In order to maximize the eclipse potential, take a look at which houses in your Natal Chart will be hosting the current eclipses. You'll have to consult an ephemeris or ask an astrologer about the signs that contain the current eclipses. Houses are the areas of experience where we meet certain energy. Most likely you will have the eclipses occur in opposing houses, but this is not always the case depending on which house system is used.

So to see which themes the eclipses will stir up, find out in which signs the eclipses are currently happening. Next, look at your chart to see where these signs are located. [*See links at the end of this book to find out how to get your chart printed.] Once you identify the houses that are being activated by the eclipses, you can read the descriptions below to discover which themes are accented. Any natal planets in close contact with the eclipses can indicate that big changes are afoot.

The houses are similar to the signs in that they hold opposing energies that are linked by some core truth. For example, the First House is about the *Self* and the house opposing it is the Seventh House, the house of *Partnership*. This gives us the theme of relationship – our relationship with ourselves and the identity we put forth versus our relationships with others. Below, I have highlighted some themes associated with each pair of opposing Houses, beginning with the First House, opposed by the Seventh House, and going around to the Sixth House–Twelfth House polarity.

Eclipses in the 1-7 Axis: Authenticity.

Themes: Self and Other; personality and appearance; your identity and outlook on life; marriage and divorce; business partners; close friends and open enemies; personal needs vs. other people's needs.

Questions: How do I present myself to others? Does my appearance match my inner self? What would I like to change about myself? What kind of relationships am I attracting? Do I sacrifice my own needs for the sake of others? Do I expect my partners to cave to my demands? What do I want/need in a committed relationship?

Eclipses in the 2-8 Axis: Being-ness.

Themes: Material possessions and security; personal income and self-value; shared income and investments; sexuality and the physical body; death and inheritance; initiation and magic.

Questions: What are my talents, skills and personal resources? How do I value myself? Am I taking care of myself financially? Do I rely on others for a sense of security? Are there hidden fears keeping me frozen? How do I relate to my sexuality? What is my relationship to death?

Eclipses in the 3-9 Axis: Exploration.

Themes: Your immediate surroundings; intellectual interests and higher education; communication, including publishing; perception and meaning; siblings and neighbors; foreign travel; your philosophy, religion or world view.

Questions: Am I over- or under-stimulated? What activities or interests help feed my mind and broaden my horizons? Are there old philosophies – the way I make sense of the world – that are ready to be evaluated and possibly changed? What is foreign, new, or unusual to me? Do I want to begin a course of study, do some traveling or learn a new skill?

Eclipses in the 4-10 Axis: Responsibility.

Themes: Home and family, including roots and ancestry; emotional core; your career; the private self and the public self; long-range goals and ambitions; authority figures; achievement.

Questions: How do I balance the personal and the professional in my life? Which one gets more attention? Are there more responsibilities I am being asked to take on at work or in the home? What do I want to achieve professionally? What unresolved family issues are ready to be addressed? How do I feel?

Eclipses in the 5-11 Axis: Social Awareness.*

Themes: Self-expression and creativity; children; the beginning of love affairs and romance; your larger social circle, friends, organizations and groups; humanitarian goals; ideals in action.

Questions: What is my relationship with my creativity? Am I ready for new romance, either in a current relationship or new encounter? Do the people I associate with share common goals and aspirations? How do I parent my children or tend to my creative projects? What is the legacy I want to leave for future generations?

Eclipses in the 6-12 Axis: Enlightened Service.*

Themes: Daily work and service; health, nutrition and the body; pets and small animals; the collective unconscious, dreams and mystical longing; karmic or past life events; solitude and spiritual service.

Questions: Am I ready to begin a new spiritual practice or re-commit to my current spiritual path? What are my dreams trying to tell me? How can I release patterns of suffering, including feelings of victimization, struggles with addictions, or detachment? What is the connection between my physical health and my emotional-spiritual health? How am I being called to serve others? How can daily rituals such as eating, sleeping and bathing bring me spiritual as well as physical nourishment? What part of my body needs healing?

*Credit for the phrases "Social Awareness" and "Enlightened Service" to describe the 5-11 axis and 6-12 axis respectively goes to astrologer Moses Siregar III. All of his descriptions for the houses can be found at his website: www.astrologyforthesoul.com.

The Phases of the Moon

Not only is the Moon changing sign and shape, it's also always changing its relationship to the Sun. This gives us its phase, an important timing tool used by ancient people as well as those still living close to natural cycles. As the Moon travels around the earth, the angle it makes to the Sun changes. This denotes the phases of the Moon, which change every 45 degrees or 3.5 days.

The Lunar Phase is an important factor in the Natal Chart as well, telling us what the template is through which we experience events and issues throughout our current lifetime. I think of it like the tint of glasses through which we see the world.

It may be interesting to find out which Lunar Phase you were born into in order to understand more about your essential nature. To do this, you would need to find out the distance between the Sun and the Moon by degrees. You can also simply follow the phases of the Moon each month and notice how you feel during each sequence. Perhaps there is a phase during which you consistently feel more productive, at east, and comfortable. This could be your Natal Lunar Phase.

There are some great books about the phases of the Moon, such as Demetra George's *Mysteries of the Dark Moon,* as well as calendars like Jim Maynard's *Pocket Astrologer* which helps you track the Moon through the signs and phases. Here, I've attempted to give only an introduction to this idea of using the phases of the Moon for personal exploration and magical practices.

Each phase of the Moon has particular themes and associations. Tuning into the phases of the Moon was something common to all agrarian peoples of the past, who knew when to plant, harvest, prune, and weed according to this Lunar calendar. Today, we can use it as well. Not only can we align ourselves with the natural rhythms of the Moon simply by observing each phase, but we can use these phases for timing and planning important events in our lives.

The Moon is in each phase for approximately 3.5 days. From New to Full, the Moon is growing in light and in its waxing phase. From just after Full to the Dark Moon, the light is decreasing and the Moon's phase is waning. You can quickly ascertain whether the Moon is waxing or waning by using your own hands. Stand outside so you are facing the direction of south. Cup your hands so that make the shape of a "C." If the Moon's roundness would fit into the "C" of your left hand, then the Moon is waning. If the rounded part fits into the cup of the right hand, then it is waxing.

Use the questions and considerations in each section to begin exploring the lunar phases on your own. The goddess associated with each phase might also provide a rich treasury of stories and symbols to guide you on a journey of self-reflection aligned with the many faces of the mysterious Moon.

New Moon: Seeds of Life

Once a month the Moon moves in between the Sun and the Earth and becomes invisible to us. This is said to be the best time to plant seeds for above-ground crops and grafting plants. For this Moon, we are still in the darkness, like seeds underground, but can sense that some change is coming. To read more about the New Moon, see pages 57-82.

Sun-Moon Angle: 0-45 degrees

Keywords: Beginnings, Innocence, Leadership, Spontaneity

Actions to take: Seeing the world with new eyes; bringing the gifts of the "other world" through; setting intentions

Goddess of this Moon: Isis, Egyptian Goddess of Resurrection who leads the dead from the underworld into new life. In her stories, she must find and re-assemble the pieces of her beloved Osiris. Together, they create the Divine Child Horus. Isis can show us too how to move into new life after we've fallen apart. She is the mother and midwife for our precious seeds of intention.

Considerations and questions for the New Moon: Are you beginning a new project? Where could you use more spontaneity? Is it time for a new perspective on your life? What could help you develop a more innocent, less cynical approach to life?

Crescent Moon: Reaching up through the soil

The Crescent Moon hangs low in the western sky just after the sun goes down. This Moon always looks sweet as a baby to me, full of promise and hope, which is one of its themes.

Sun-Moon Angle: 46-90 degrees

Keywords: Family, Culture of origin, Hope, Desire

Actions to take: Making choices that generate confidence; overcoming habits; acknowledging the tension between your ideals and the mundane world.

Goddess of this Moon: Selene, Greek Goddess of the Moon who falls in love with a mortal and puts a spell on him so that he never dies or grows old. But the spell means that he must sleep forever. Although Selene bears many children and is much loved, her own love is imprisoned in unconsciousness. Working with Selene means uncovering our desires and working to manifest them in more conscious ways.

Considerations and questions for the Crescent Moon: What makes you feel hopeful and lifts your spirits? What are the values and themes you associate with your family of origin? Are they the right values for your life? What kind of changes do you hunger to make in the world?

First Quarter Moon: Establishing Roots & Branches

The First Quarter Moon shines high in the sky around sunset. Sometimes referred to as a "half-moon," its shape resembles a pie cut in half. The First Quarter Moon marks a time to understand how our intentions are beginning to take shape in the world, and what that means for ourselves and others.

Sun-Moon Angle: 91-135 degrees

Keywords: Will power, Sacrifice for larger goals, Acknowledging the tension between self and other.

Actions to take: Taking charge of the situation; making a break from the past; laying the groundwork for one's personal beliefs.

Goddess of this Moon: Durga is the Hindu Goddess who slays a demon in order to restore peace to all the worlds. She is the fierce, active principle of compassion. Durga takes on the impossible and reveals the impermanence of life.

Considerations and questions for the Firth Quarter Moon: Astrologer Dane Rudhyar calls this phase the "crisis of will in action." It's a time to make something happen. When life hands you an impossible task, what's one small step you can take to move forward? What are the ways your past is holding you back? Is it time to learn the art of compromise or stand your ground?

Gibbous Moon: Budding

The waxing Gibbous Moon brings the energy of anticipation. We are nearing a time of culmination, when we may see the fruits of our past labors. We can use this time to see if there are any last-minute alterations we need to make to our plans. The Gibbous Moon is a good time to put together the finishing touches, whether that means editing or adding to the vision.

Sun-Moon Angle: 136-180

Keywords: Refining, Fine-tuning, Competency

Actions to take: Giving and receiving support; building the structures to achieve goals; perfecting one's mission

Goddess of this Moon: The High Priestess is a sacred role taken by women throughout many times and cultures to bring the Goddess down to Earth. The High Priestess carries dual consciousness of the Divine and the Mundane and can teach us how to bridge these two spheres of life.

Considerations and questions for the Gibbous Moon: It's time to get clear about what you want. Anything extraneous or superfluous will get blown out of proportion when the Full Moon hits. Where could you simplify things? Are there any goals or projects you need to re-think or review? Can you ask for help when you need it?

Full Moon: Fruit and Flower

The Full Moon rises in the east just as the Sun is setting in the west. It is a time of heightened energy and illumination. Sometimes the intensity sheds light on accomplishments, while at other times the glare seems to hit our every blemish and imperfection. With this Moon, we imagine fruits and flowers at their peak of vitality. For more on the Full Moon, see pages 83-100.

Sun-Moon Angle: 181-225

Keywords: Manifestation, Ovulation, Fulfillment, Celebration

Actions to take: Seeking connection to others; feeling and acting from the height of one's power; creating outward expressions of self

Goddess of this Moon: Inanna, Queen of Heaven, Earth and the Underworld. She is the Sumerian Goddess who creates culture, art and the very roots of civilization. Inanna is both a trickster, laughing at adversity, and a goddess who undergoes serious and sometimes painful transformations in order to manifest her wholeness.

Considerations and questions for the Full Moon: Each Full Moon is an opportunity to celebrate the accomplishments from the previous month. At the same time, if there is anything overwhelming or out of control in your life, this would be a good time to release yourself from those negative influences. What are your grateful for in your life?

Disseminating Moon: Gathering the Harvest

The Disseminating Moon is said to be the best time for planting root crops and perennials. It appears on the eastern horizon later in the night. It is a Moon for sharing, relating, and teaching in order to strengthen our connections to others.

Sun-Moon Angle: 226-270

Keywords: Teaching, Harvesting, Communication

Actions to take: Releasing what's been created; sharing the fruits of one's labors; facing the consequences of past actions; helping others

Goddess of this Moon: Ceres is the Roman Goddess of harvest and grain. She knows the time to reap and shares her bounty with the people. In one myth, she loses her daughter Proserpina to the underworld, and wanders in grief with a lighted torch until her daughter's return. Her story shows the need to process emotions and withdraw from life at times in order to make clear a way forward.

Considerations and questions for the Disseminating Moon: After the intense experiences of the Full Moon, we return home with the wisdom gained from our experiences. What wisdom do you have to share with others in your life? How can you be supportive to others in your community? If you have recently encountered difficulties, what do you need to do to repair the damage or return to a state of health?

Last Quarter Moon: Decomposing

The Last Quarter Moon is the time of reckoning and reconciling. We have gathered so much at this point on the wheel, and we can sense that a new cycle is approaching. This is a good time to integrate the lessons of the past in order to see what works and what needs adjustment.

Sun-Moon Angle: 271-315

Keywords: Receiving feedback, Service and ritual, Re-evaluation

Actions to take: Allowing new insights to cause a re-organization of one's consciousness; transcending the limitations of the material world; letting go of old forms; releasing what no longer has relevance or value

Goddess of this Moon: Changing Woman is a central goddess to the Diné people. As the year proceeds, she changes from young to old but is powerful enough to reverse the process when spring comes again. Changing Woman is a goddess who created humanity out of her own skin when she became lonely. She teaches us how to move through the changes of life creatively and to deal with surprises as they arrive without worrying about what's to come.

Considerations and questions for the Last Quarter Moon: Astrologer Dane Rudhyar calls this Moon the "crisis of consciousness," and we are aligned with this phase anytime we are pushed to the edges of our understanding. As a symbol of changing how we think and feel about the world, use it to contemplate how you are being forced to update your perception. Are there new philosophies, ideas or spiritual principles that you would like to put in place? What new information has been uncomfortable for you to deal with?

Basalmic Moon: Into the Dark

The Basalmic or Dark Moon is the Crone's Moon, a time for deep introspection and withdrawal into the self. At the same time, this a great Moon for connecting with the others worlds, for asking for spiritual guidance and healing. Attention goes to the process and the unseen rather than the material facets of existence.

Sun-Moon Angle: 316-360

Keywords: Completion, Death, The Invisible, The Mystic

Actions to take: Opening to or reinforcing one's psychic abilities; surrendering the ego; turning inward to distill the central meanings of life; tending to and finishing up the works of the past; remembering

Goddess of this Moon: The Morrigan is a terrifying goddess in Celtic traditions. She is the Goddess of Death, Prophecy and Endings. She teaches how to face change and find a way to see into the future even when life seems darkest.

Considerations and questions for the Basalmic/Dark Moon: Just as compost makes good soil for new growth, so the Dark Moon beckons us to return to our essence in order to prepare the way forward. What are the things about yourself or your life that could use to be composted? How does your darkness relate to your creativity? How do you support yourself when you need to reflect, restore, or release?

The Moon in Our Time

Maybe at this point you are thinking, *Who has time to honor every single Full Moon or set intentions every New Moon?* Maybe you're thinking that this is all nice in theory, but the practice of tracking the Moon or journaling about our feelings seems like just one more thing to add onto an already taxing to-do list. Maybe you're ready to put the book down and just get back to work. If so, then these next few pages are for you.

They're for me, too. For most of my life I have felt caught between the desire for depth, connection and self-awareness on one end and the urge to make something useful, to feel important and to get recognition for what I do. Now, there's nothing wrong with wanting to feel important or receive recognition. It only becomes a problem when the latter takes over entirely and the former is left by the side of the road to beg for scraps.

Before, during and after any journey, we need to consider who we are, where we come from and what has nurtured and informed us so far. In the pause, we reconnect with the original impulse or desire which drew us onto the road in the first place. The Moon lives in the pause. In the preceding pages, we looked at ways to take action on the New and Full Moons. Now let's examine why that might be important.

In the language of astrology, the Moon is often linked with the Feminine, while other planets such as the Sun, Saturn or Mars are linked with the Masculine. When we speak of "masculine" and "feminine" qualities here, we are not necessarily talking about gender. The conventional binary gender system would have us ascribe "masculine" to men and "feminine" to women, but the past few decades are educating us in how these qualities are at play in each one of us. We need to understand that female-socialized people will often display more "feminine" qualities and vice versa for male-socialized people. This can be useful in determining which qualities or attributes are valued and which are devalued as a whole by our largely masculine-centric culture. There are certain situations in which using a binary gender system can be useful, but like any system it is also limiting.

Generally when I use the terms Masculine and Feminine they are descriptions of archetypal qualities at work in each one of us.

Let me give some definitions so we are on the same page. The Masculine polarity can be described as outward-oriented, active and fast-moving. It is the outer world of manifestation and action. It is the future. It is intellect and spirit. Time here is linear and goal-oriented. The Feminine polarity is inward-oriented, receptive and slow-moving. It is the inner world of the formless, the imagination, the memory, the soul and the body. It is intuitive. Time here is often focused more on the past than the future. Feminine time is also cyclical, a spiral which never ends.

Again, the Moon is Feminine in polarity and so is associated with the qualities of the Feminine. In learning how to work with the Moon, we are learning how to listen to the deep voice within each one of us. It might feel daunting to add it to that aforementioned to-do list, but honoring and consciously expressing the Moon in our time may just be a key ingredient to changing our collective story and evolving human culture.

As an example from very recent history, let's look at the Occupy Wall Street movement, which began on September 17, 2011, in Liberty Square in Manhattan's financial district and quickly spread across the United States and the world as a collective cry against greed. People camped out in freezing temperatures and withstood police threats and violence in order to carry out large scale demonstrations against the rule of the so-called 1%. In the language of archetypes, such activities seem very Masculine: outward oriented, fast-moving and active. But the way these movements manifested was decidedly Feminine in nature. Just look at how it was described in the press: *They have no message. They are too broad. They are too inclusive. What do they really want? It's confusing and messy. They're just feeding people and taking care of addicts, and the mentally ill.*

Many were uncomfortable that those who usually lived on the edges of society now had a central place of convergence. This meant that more of us had to see the gravity and severity of income inequality, lack of services and the widespread epidemic of homelessness and poverty. It may be easy to ignore that one person with a sign asking for spare change, but what about a whole camp of people who have been victimized, marginalized or ignored by a disconnected, dysfunctional culture?

To some members of the media, the Occupy movements were confusing, had no clear message and seemed too broad and inclusive to get anything done. To drive home the point, reporters would sometimes highlight the nightly General Conferences, where people gathered to speak and use consensus-based tools to reach decisions. In each Occupy camp, a leaderless, process-oriented, democratic consensus practice would happen every evening at 7:00 P.M. to discuss problems, decide on strategy and build community between participants. Sometimes it looked like nothing got accomplished in these meetings. People shared life stories. They talked about disputes in the camps themselves. They brought up sanitation issues. They decided on working agreements for keeping the camps safe and functioning. The meetings may have been dismissed by a confused public or the mainstream media because it was so outside of our usual way of being in the world. What could a bunch of riffraff on the streets really accomplish? Well, here are a few examples:

- Occupy the Farm and Occupy Berkeley have created a farm from vacant land, allowing previously unused space to be accessible and beneficial to the local community.
- The Occupy movement has shifted the national dialogue to discussing issues of social inequality.
- The encampments that characterized the movement during Fall 2011 enabled formerly disparate and disconnected groups of people to build vast in-person and online networks.
- Encampments across the country have fed and clothed local homeless populations despite scant resources.
- Occupy Providence struck a deal with the city to open a homeless shelter during the winter that would also provide social services.
- Occupy Our Homes, a national coalition of Occupy-affiliated groups, has stopped numerous illegal foreclosures across the country.

What is this brief synopsis of the occupy movement doing in a book about the Astrological Moon? Notice all the things that Occupy was, well, occupied with creating: safe space, access to food, affordable housing, shelter for the vulnerable, policies based on relationships, social equality. These themes are also topics very directly related to the themes ruled over by the Astrological Moon. Occupy movements were showing us what modern society has been sorely lacking: the messy, complex, inclusive, process-oriented, feeling, nurturing Feminine.

It happens that when we over-identify with something while summarily dismissing its opposite, we lose sight of what both things really are. In order to survive and succeed in a culture that defines itself primarily through masculine qualities, we become super-masculine. When this happens, in addition to losing our connection to the feminine within us, we lose clarity about what the masculine truly is as well.

What is the Masculine archetype? What is its purpose? In Jungian psychology, the Masculine energy in each person is supposed to "protect the realm," to serve the inner-world, which is the domain of the divine or inner Feminine. But all too often in our world, the Masculine ends up violating it. These violations can occur from outside forces such as partners, families, armies, corporations or other entities. They can also be self-inflicted. Any time we betray the sacred within us, our Masculine archetype has forgotten its job.

When the sacred is separated from the secular, then the outer world becomes the only source of meaning. The Masculine then looks outside itself for the next conquest or validation of self-worth. When we push the sacred out, we are sacrificing meaning – which is actually the only thing that may have a chance of sustaining us throughout life's ups and downs.

The Masculine stays purposefully unconscious by overextending, focusing on "outer world" concerns, achievements and the products we make. Again, this leads to a lack of meaning. Don't get me wrong, I am in favor of action, achievement and tangible results. We need the Masculine part of us; it is a vitalizing energy. But action for the sake of action is a by-product of our resistance to the Feminine. Over-extending ourselves, taking on too much responsibility and workaholic tendencies – this sort of pattern keeps us unaware of what is going on inside of us. The pace of our society can fool us into believing that we are happy. The word "happiness" is related to the verb "to happen." Happiness is a state of presence to what is happening. To what portion of our days can we say with sincerity that we are truly present?

When our Moon is under-served, it becomes agitated. We begin to feel restless, moody and dissatisfied. We seek comforts to numb us out. Thus numbed, we think everything is okay. Some part of us knows that if we allow uncomfortable feelings to continue we will have to question our motivations, the very meaning of life. It makes sense that we don't often seek out the Feminine.

We've just spent a few centuries really honing our ability to banish the Feminine energy. Simultaneously, we've been trained to sharpen our masculine energy for outer world battles and conquests without regard to its sacred duty. Now another way opens before us. Now we can resume the quest to remember and evolve that part of us.

Whether facing painful feelings, changing careers or attempting to honor the Moon by reading some book, it's important to remember that there's no getting it right. There is only facing what is within us with love and acceptance. If we can let our Masculine side remember who he serves, perhaps the core essence of who we are will be revealed. But it will only happen by embracing the unpredictable, messy, confusing and uncontrollable parts of ourselves. A slow-moving, inward process of transformation can become a compass that shows us the way to go into a new life. It takes patience.

Noticing the Moon in the sky, taking time for rituals, making space for the sacred, becoming aware of what you need, paying attention to your emotions – these things are radical acts. Don't try to do everything. Be grateful for any way these ideas surface in your life. They are the seeds of the revolution.

Now that the Occupy movements are "over," the press and pundits can point out their failures. More accurately, they can forget the entire episode. But here's the surprise folks: the movements aren't over. They have simply evolved. The Occupy Wall Street (OWS) organization was instrumental to getting aid, resources and information out to people who were affected by Hurricane Sandy. Members of the New York National Guard were actually being trained and coordinated by the good people of the OWS. Chapters of Occupy continue to meet all across the country, supporting people who are fighting foreclosure, feeding the homeless and organizing for more services for the mentally ill. The movement isn't over. It keeps going, quietly doing the work that needs to be done. (Remind you of anyone's mother?)

The point is that the Feminine isn't interested in succeeding, not the way Western Civilization is. Our society has canonized success in the outer world as sacred – making money, building an empire, winning wars. At this parade of feats, the Feminine simply yawns. She wants to know how you feel. She wants to know if you are being true to yourself. She wants to know what's left after all the glory fades and you are in your darkest hours, despairing over lost love. She wants to see all of you. She knows that failure, not variety, is the spice of life. Failure is a doorway to authenticity. It lets us discover the part of us that deserves love regardless of what we have or haven't accomplished. It is such a fundamental aspect of our human-ness, and it takes great courage to face.

Running Towards Failure

"I am desperately running towards what anyone in their right mind would be running away from. Which is femaleness, which is failure."

~ Eileen Myles, poet

I've spent over half my life as a self-identified witch and have devoted my professional life to empowering women's voices. So it came as a shock to me when, at the age of 37, I encountered my own strong resistance to the Feminine. As my marriage of 7 years began showing cracks and wounds too painful to ignore, my instincts were to blame my husband and run away.

I confronted him late one night, after our children were asleep. I had pulled some Tarot cards earlier in the evening to get guidance about how to proceed, and I had to admit that the cards for leaving him looked a lot more promising.

He sat down on the sofa next to me and asked me if something was wrong. I told him, "This can't go on," and offered an inventory of his lack of self-love and his broken commitments to take care of himself emotionally and spiritually. These complaints may have been valid, but in the midst of my own pain I was unwilling to see my role in the breakdown. His apologies and promises to change did little to reassure me in the moment.

I didn't want to admit it then, but my own inner-Masculine had been running amok. Because I serve the Goddess, go to therapy regularly, and work almost exclusively with women, I let myself fall under the illusion that my own inner-Feminine was well-tended. But looks can be deceiving.

For the next few months, I had to face my own prejudices against the Feminine, leaving me confused and uttering, "What, me?!" I began to see more clearly the power my inner masculine voices had over me – those that demand action and chide me for my own over-sensitivity, those that judge my self-worth based on an impossible definition of responsibility. I confused having responsibility with being the "sole authority." I sought control over my life at any cost, even if it meant essentially objectifying my own husband's masculinity and denying his feminine side.

I had been shutting down his emotions and then blaming him, unaware that I was really running away from the healing I myself desperately wanted. I was so afraid of appearing to fail that I almost sacrificed this relationship to pursue my own objectives, thinking I could do it better "on my own" – and worse, that *not* doing it on my own meant that I was potentially weak. Was I the one lacking in self-love, failing to take care of my own emotional and spiritual needs?

Failure is such a dirty word in much of the Western world, and I think our refusal to acknowledge the importance of failure is our refusal to acknowledge the value of the Feminine.

As the world entered the year 2011, revolution and upheaval seemed to sweep the globe. Notions of success and failure came up again and again, in discussions of the Occupy Movements, the Arab Spring and the continued fight for women's rights in the U.S. With so much at stake, these terms deserved to be revisited. For me, the task of re-examining assumptions about success and failure was inherently connected to the Masculine and Feminine archetypes – the God and the Goddess within each of us. Learning what these ideas and terms mean to us now seems like a vital step in our evolution.

See, I am rooting for women all over the world on the frontlines of revolutionary movements, and I am working for social change in my own life. Yet again and again, I end up feeling defeated when women are shut out of the new orders that emerge after the protests, or they held to standards so different from those of their male counterparts. But in my very own life, I've placed a higher value on Masculine attributes and then wondered why I struggle so much with issues of self-worth and power. "As within, so without," the saying goes. The outer world shows us the inner world, and vice versa.

One day I realized that I had taken a beautiful line of poetry from the "Charge of the Star Goddess" and turned it into a weapon wielded with precision within me. The invocation, written as if spoken by the Goddess, tells us at one point, "If that which you seek, you find not within yourself, you will never find it without."

I would use this as a kind of threat, the voice in my head full of vitriol and judgment, *"Hey, Rhea, have you found it yet? Spiritual enlightenment? An end to your anger/self-loathing/depression? The solution to your marriage issues? Are you embodying the Goddess yet? Well, what are you waiting for? Get to it!"* We could do so much to heal suffering by understanding the true nature of the Masculine and Feminine, and valuing the sacred duty each has to fulfill. Rather than either/or, we could have yes/and.

Inside of me, one limited version of Masculinity doesn't want healing; it wants challenges and conquests and achievements. When I look at the world around me, it's easy to blame imbalance and injustice on a culture that cuts itself off from the sacred. But what about me? I'm supposed to know better.

In my own life, whenever I over-identify with the accomplishments of the outer-world, I lose touch with the essential nature within me as well as the sacred role of the Masculine to protect and serve that essence. When my own Masculine forgets its true purpose, instead of being a protector I become a bully. Afraid of the unknown, I lash out at anything that threatens my own desire for control and order. When I cry out at images of violence in the larger world, I am getting a call to check in with myself as well as the larger cultural environment.

How am I failing to serve my own inner-Feminine when it demands that something surrender and be changed?

These days when I hear the voice within say, "Look at how you failed," I immediately translate it to, "How is this outcome different from what I expected? What have I learned from this? What is truly important now?" It is often my failures that help me reconnect to the essence of who I am.

Almost a year after that serious conversation with my husband, we were out for a rare evening of uninterrupted conversation and dinner. As we stepped outside to breathe in the chill of the night air, I looked up into the darkness and asked him what sustains him in times of challenge.

After a few intentionally ridiculous answers, such as "Pro-wrestling," and "Lapel pins," he replied, "Us."

I playfully pushed him off balance and said, "Yeah, but what else? There's more than just us."

He looked at me and answered, "Maybe. But maybe it's all about what is created when things come together. The magic and mystery of relationship, of connection. I like the people you and I help each other be, you know?"

I needed to hear this. I need to remember this. This is why I sought out images of the Goddess in the first place, and why I circle around her again and again. Relationships, connection, there's more to life than just me.

And maybe when we take time to just bask in the Moon's presence, we awaken an inner-knowing that there's no getting it right, that there's nothing we have to do to deserve love. We are each worthy of love because we exist, and in the end it is those connections that sustain us through hard times – not the money, fame or status we may have achieved.

I need a lot of reminders of this, which is why I have spent a lot of my life Moon-gazing and charting the course of the Moon through her phases.

What does it mean to run toward failure? It doesn't mean that I want to do things badly. It means that I am taking risks, following my heart, allowing myself to be vulnerable and living as authentically as possible, all the while knowing that I may not end up in the place I want to be. I may end up somewhere else. Failure can then be re-defined as an unexpected outcome. Instead of the antithesis of success, it is the unlikely destination we arrive at when we have allowed ourselves to be affected by the journey itself.

Slowly – and with both great effort and surrender – I am discovering that this is the way to move through uncertain times and embrace the gifts of failure. And this is why we may want to spend even a little bit of time tending to our own hearts or honoring an occasional Full Moon. The pause from action gives us a chance to reassess and take stock of what we've learned so far on this crazy life adventure. We make an altar, write intentions or spend time building intimacy with a loved one – and maybe we discover that we are on a totally different trajectory. Or maybe we realize that we are in exactly the right time and place. Perhaps it is the pause that takes us deeper and makes real and lasting revolution possible, in a heart or a marriage, or the larger world.

Part III. The Moon in the Natal Chart

The moon, like a flower
In heaven's high bower,
With silent delight
Sits and smiles on the night.

~ William Blake

Creating a more sustainable, just and peaceful planet depends upon each one of us deepening our understanding of ourselves and our world. In western cultures especially, we are cut off from our bodies and from our emotions. From examples of super-thin female bodies or muscular male bodies, to the marketing of various substances that control our feelings, from consumerism and the valuing of selfishness, to the lack of art and music instruction in public schools, we are taught again and again that the body and the emotions are something to be avoided if possible and, barring that, at least managed and subdued.

When we lose a sense of relationship to our own bodies and feelings, the way we relate to each other and our world is altered. Without clearly understanding our own inner landscapes, we create outer landscapes that are built on projections, shadows and unexpressed needs.

This is especially true as it relates to the changing, emotional moon. It is through respecting one's emotional needs that one can create a solid base on which to build clear, strong goals for life. When you know what your body needs and what you are feeling, you are no longer imprisoned by those things. As astrologer Caroline Casey writes in *Making the Gods Work for You*, "Moods are messengers." If we fail to listen, we lose out on the wisdom they have for us.

As both a great cosmic signpost and symbolic language of the psyche, astrology helps us uncover patterns in our lives – some patterns we like, some not so much. Astrology is not static, but alive. It doesn't necessarily tie us to any fate, although it does insist that we work through certain issues. I like to play with the idea that before each person is born, the soul-part draws up the natal chart, choosing the moment of birth in order to create the best map to follow through life. When we remember our mission, we are following our own personal roadmap and encountering the kinds of experiences we need to have this time around on Planet Earth.

In this section, we will be looking at the Moon in each of the signs of the zodiac. At its most basic, the astrological Moon represents our inner nature. The Moon by sign, house and aspect can help us answer vital questions such as:

- How do I give and receive love?
- What are my natural defense mechanisms?
- What am I looking for in relationships?
- What do I need to feel supported?

Wherever the Moon was when you were born will reveal how you manifest these vital energies and who you are when no one's looking. To find out which sign the Moon was in when you were born, see Appendix A in the back of this book for information on accessing your very own Natal Chart.

GENERAL THEMES OF THE ASTROLOGICAL MOON

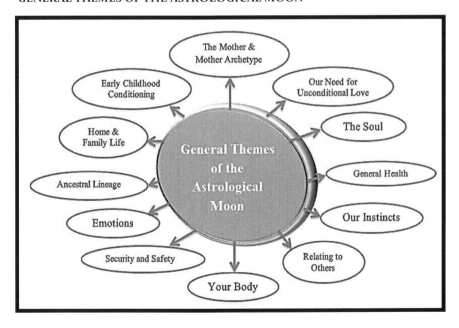

Learning to Love

Often the Moon illuminates how we were nurtured as children and what kind of energies shaped the early childhood environment. This early conditioning has a tremendous effect on how we nurture others and ourselves in later life. Investigating the Moon in our Natal Charts gives us insight into our relationships with caregivers and the ways we were given or denied access to the security we craved. Only by careful examination and acceptance of where we came from can we open to loving, new relationships with others as adults.

As a symbol of the watery feminine, the Moon also tells us about the archetype of The Mother. On the spiritual level, the Moon is the Great Mother Goddess, who shines her love and support on all her children. Here, Mother is about resourcefulness, compassion, and generosity.

In psychological terms, the Mother Archetype is often associated with the word *sacrifice*, the requirement that for something to receive what it needs, another thing must make do with less. There is some truth in this, as no one can give an unlimited amount of energy to another without depleting their own. But it is also true that the Moon, which reflects the light of the Sun, gives its radiance to Earth without detriment to itself.

The roots for the word *sacrifice* come from the Latin *sacrificus* and *facere* which mean *to perform sacred rites*. The meaning of *giving up something for the sake of another* doesn't come into common usage until the 16th Century. At its core, honoring the Moon means performing the sacred rites we know are essential to our emotional and physical well-being.

For both men and women, connecting with the original meaning of this word and uncovering the ways our Moon connects us to the Feminine or Goddess aspect within each of us eventually leads us closer toward manifesting love and support in our lives. Through your Moon Sign, you will see how to tap into your own Divine essence and release some lunar magic into your world. Often this means giving yourself the kind of mothering you desired as a child and still crave as an adult.

By looking at the Moon's sign, house and aspects in your birth chart, you will find out how you can use the natural resources of your Moon placements to your benefit in all aspects of your life. This book is a great place to begin the journey of self-acceptance that leads to greater happiness. Respecting your emotional needs will create a solid base on which to build clear, strong goals for the rest of your life.

The next few chapters will take you on a tour of the Moon by Sign, House and Aspect. In each Moon Sign, you will discover the strengths, the shadows and the art of relationships pertaining to the energies of each sign. As I worked on writing these sections, specific goddesses began showing up to give me their input. After a while, I finally got the message to sit with each of them and let their voices come through my writing. This process imparted a special message channeled directly from a specific goddess associated with the energy of that sign. In some cases, I had to push aside my own thoughts on whether this goddess was really right for a certain sign. In the end, I gave in and trusted that even if the goddess wasn't an immediate fit in my own mind, they obviously had something valuable to offer for further exploration and integration. These passages of channeled information are offered as a way to tap into the Divine within you.

The Moon through the Signs of the Zodiac

The seasonal zodiac used by Western Astrologers begins each spring with Aries and circles around the twelve signs to Pisces. At their most basic, the **signs of the zodiac** represent qualities of being – such as *playful, curious, stubborn*, or *compassionate*. They tell us how we will express the various archetypal energies of the Planets.

The **sign** that the Moon is in when a person is born offers us insight about that individual's feeling nature and the ways they instinctively seek security and comfort. It can help us to understand the Mother archetype as we experienced it and the conditions of early childhood, as well as what each person needs to be aware of to create a secure home and healthy relationships as a result of that legacy. The Moon Sign clarifies the gifts and attributes that a person naturally possesses. These are the essential ways we share or withhold our reservoir of power.

While the Moon is archetypally feminine, I want it to be crystal clear that it is a part of each one of us. The Feminine is typically defined as receptive, changing, intuitive, cyclical and watery. Every human, regardless of gender, has an inner femme: a source of watery, changing, flowing mystery that we need to acknowledge in order to be whole.

I have used the pronoun *you* throughout the sections on the Moon by sign, house and aspect in a desire to be inclusive of all genders without having to go the confusing he/she/they route.

In focusing on a specific goddess to connect with at the end of each Moon-sign section, my intention is not to exclude any gender, but to help each of us accept the Feminine aspects that live within. We need to allow the Feminine part of us to reassert its importance, value and wisdom in our world. It starts with you. Learning about your Moon Sign can begin this journey of accepting your inner feminine nature, as well as discovering a more authentic and vibrant life.

Moon in Aries

- Your Natural Resource: Strength
- Your Art of Loving: Reclaiming wilderness
- The Dark Side of the Moon: Love is a battlefield
- The Goddess Within: Artemis

Fiery and raw, the Moon in Aries is the wilderness. This Moon leads to places where human logic and rationales come up against the pure instinctual energy of nature: creation and destruction, aggression and desire. This Moon is a furnace and bestows the natural resources of independence and strength.

The inner power of an Aries Moon is power itself. It may not matter which way the wind is blowing, only that it is blowing at all. It is in action and movement that security is found; in changing, a sense of stability.

Aries is often called headstrong, but in a sense, if you have the Moon in Aries, you may often feel ruled by your heart and emotions. An impulse arises that gets you excited – it could be an idea, a feeling or a desire – and then you leap into action. The Moon really plays this up, pushing you to act from this instinctual level. Ruled by the angry red planet Mars, an Aries Moon can be seen as combative and domineering in relationships. But when you remember to let your natural strength and power flow, you are incredibly devoted to your friends and family. How you let that power flow is by taking bold actions that allow you to master your own destiny, while still leaving plenty of room for others to make their own decisions.

With your Moon here, you came into this world with a clear notion of what you want. But when you attach your whole identity to a specific person, idea or philosophy, you set yourself up for intense disappointment and frustration. The Aries Moon could learn to see strength as described in the wise Tao te Ching: *Yield and overcome. Bend and be straight. Empty and be full.*

The Moon tells us about how we can create a home environment that aligns with our deeper selves. The home of an Aries Moon might resemble something out of ancient Sparta, with an obvious lack of accessories and an emphasis on simplicity. This is because you may be so busy that you don't have time to pay attention to how your home looks. But a desire for change could just as easily lead to endless home improvement projects that never get finished or other urges to constantly upgrade.

You need to remember that you came here to embody your natural resource of strength, and that means being ready for action. Responding to the moment is often easier when you aren't bogged down with too much stuff. It could be easy for an Aries Moon to acquire "the next best thing" out of an unconscious desire to keep up with the demands of life. But you may actually want more simplicity and utility than you think. The excitement of new exercise equipment or complicated camping gear could just be covering up a more natural inclination for agility.

You need a home that won't block your natural power and strength. If you have too much to take care of, you could easily fall into a cycle of irresponsibility, causing you to make rash decisions or to ignore smaller problems that then become long-term regrets.

Relationships and the Art of Loving:
Reclaiming Wilderness

With the Moon in Aries, the mother or other primary caregiver may have been a powerful protector in childhood or a volcano ready to explode. Expressing anger in the home may have caused much family turmoil, but withholding it was just as dangerous as letting it out.

The Aries Moon may indicate that you had to compete for affection and attention from caregivers. Whether through friendly encouragement or outright intimidation, caregivers may have helped ignite the fiery raw energy of your Aries Moon. Early experiences of competition may have taught you how to be independent and not let anything get in the way of what they want. However, you may have taken the brunt of some pretty harsh expectations of achievement and success.

In this way, you inherited a tricky mixture to balance in your relationships when it comes to self-esteem. You may pin all your self-worth on doing the best, being first or getting the most. But you also know what you want and aren't afraid to ask for it. Although this can look selfish to others, it is because of an instinctive sensitivity to others and a strong intuition that you are able to make such demands from life.

When an Aries Moon spreads its roots into the core knowledge that you have a unique gift to bring the world and that you are the master of your own destiny, you can let go of having to be right. You can let go of an infantile need to enforce rules on others as well. Just like a seed bursting forth from fertile soil in the spring, the mighty power that directs you also connects you to others. Its power is the essence of life itself.

Because the Moon in Aries is working from instinct, you may have an unconscious expectation for your friends, partners and other loved ones to know what they want and take it. Being unassertive may be seen as weakness or deficiency, and a lack of action frustrates the Aries Moon. Other times, you may be looking for clues about who you are in the actions and words of other people. Attaching to another then becomes a matter of self-preservation: Other people become a part of the Moon in Aries' identity. If other people fail, the Aries Moon individual also feels like a failure for choosing them.

With the Moon in Aries, you need someone who is as strong as you are, so you can meet the challenges of life with vitality and brilliance. Just remember that strength comes in many different flavors, sizes and colors.

The art of loving, for an Aries Moon, means accepting your own wild nature and working with it consciously. When you embrace your inner strength, you can learn to dance with your instincts and still have respectful relationships. Cultivating thoughtful awareness of your emotions often means finding personally fulfilling outlets for your power. When you satisfy that inner wilderness, you create more space for the people you love to be who they are. You also take the pressure off your close relationships to be the sole source of fire and passion.

The Dark Side of the Moon: Love is a Battlefield

The Moon in Aries displays two faces of archetypal feminine and masculine principles coming to a head: the desire for connection (the feminine Moon) and the desire to assert individuality (the masculine Mars). The desire for a fight springs from the feeling that for things to be real and worthy of devotion, they must be tested in the heat of battle. A little competition and argument can help settle who's right, which then gives the Aries Moon a feeling of security.

You want to feel vital and potent, able to take charge of life. There is a fated quality to this Moon, as though you have been put here for a specific reason that only you can carry out, if only you could remember what that was. It is this intangible quality of special-ness that leads you to work from your instincts and trust the rawness of your actions. But it could lead to imposing your point of view on others to the extent that other people feel lost or battered by your desires.

Channeling your intuition and energy consciously rather than letting your desires get the better of you is a big challenge of the Aries Moon. This Moon can lead you quickly to anger, frustration, depression and even rage if it is out of balance. You are here to work on balancing this raw power with your changing emotional states.

At times, the Moon in Aries may have to compromise smaller needs for the sake of larger goals, especially if you want healthy, loving relationships. Finding ways to channel that raw power outside of your relationships – such as participating in athletic teams, martial arts, or other healthy outlets for competition – not only feeds this Moon, but helps keep the edge out of your relationships. Make a commitment to participate in appropriate outlets for your physical strength and vitality. A healthy sex life can also provide balance to an Aries Moon. Just be sure that you aren't making impossible demands on lovers.

Even though you exude confidence in many situations, an Aries Moon may struggle internally with self-doubt. You may not understand why you do the things you do. You just do them. Because you are often acting from instinct and can't necessarily explain why to others, you tend to get defensive and overreact whenever you are challenged.

To move out of the darkness and into the light, the Moon in Aries must strive to not take things so personally. Lashing out at loved ones may give you an immediate surge of power, but it inevitably zaps you of vitality. When a feeling arises, taking the time to feel it – without *becoming* it and without directing it all at one person – calms the destructive fires of an Aries Moon. This takes practice, as well as a desire to be free from patterns of suffering that have become a part of your identity.

The Goddess Within: Artemis

This is the Moon of the Goddess Artemis, the ancient Lady of the Beasts, running naked and free in the wilderness. As a symbol, she is full of contradiction. She is both a protector of animals and a hunter. She is both a virgin goddess and the one who calls her worshippers to the forests for wild rites of lovemaking. She claims full authority over herself and yet is ruled by pure instinct and natural law. Artemis is a reminder that forcefully using one's power will change others, but true power changes us from within.

She speaks:

"There is a time for everything. I love life but am no stranger to death. I know when it is time to sow the seeds of life, but I also know when it is time to reap. The hunter must intimately know and understand the animal he slays. In this way, he becomes the animal. The animal gives up its life, but the energy is transferred again and again. I run free to show you that the only true bond is the soul's desire, and desire springs from all that has come before it.

"Strength is not about right or wrong, but about opening your whole self to the moment. Immortality is not "never-changing" but is the continuous dance of power from one story to another, from one person to another, from one form to another. In this way, you are eternal, even when all you have is this moment."

EXPLORATION

When feelings and desires run freely through an Aries Moon, it's easier to see where the natural power wants to be directed and to be that spark of change you were born to ignite.

The Moon in Aries came here to be an example of strength. When you tap into that natural resource, you show others how to live life without fear. In small and big ways, these acts of loving bravery help to create a world that you truly love.

To find out more about the power of the goddess within you, explore these suggestions and questions:

Where do you find the wilderness in your life?

Do you feed your furnace of desire, or deny its intensity?

Can you trust your instincts and still let others have their say?

What does strength look like to you?

Moon in Taurus

- Your Natural Resource: Security
- Your Art of Loving: Defining self-worth
- The Dark Side of the Moon: Hooked on a feeling
- The Goddess Within: Hathor

A Taurus Moon's natural resource is security, which is supported by a loving awareness of nature and a connection to the green, living Earth. With the Moon here, you can tap into your inner power whenever you take time to feel grounded in your body and connected to the larger body of the Earth. Aligning yourself with this power gives you the ability to provide ease and comfort for the people you love and to delight in your own senses.

When your Moon in Taurus is balanced, you gain the ability to create pleasure and abundance no matter what life throws at you. You intuitively understand the depth and beauty of loved ones, building relationships based on interdependence rather than dependence. As you journey even deeper within, you can discover a natural gift for creating environmentally respectful practices that allow the flourishing of all life.

The Moon in Taurus says, "The body is a temple." Honoring the Moon means honoring one's body and respecting the natural systems that sustain all life on Earth. Taurus is ruled by the planet Venus, Goddess of Love and Beauty, and the Moon delights in its placement here. Traditional astrologers would say the Moon is exalted in Taurus, receiving the resources and recognition it deserves.

With the Moon in Taurus, you find inner security by paying attention to your body and senses. You find comfort in fully experiencing the things that sustain life – food, shelter, clothing, the elements and the seasons. These basic needs will be creatively transformed by your super sensual nature, and with this, you have the potential to discover pleasure in the most mundane places.

The Moon tells us about how we can create a home environment that aligns with our deeper selves. The ideal home for the Moon in Taurus is full of natural light and green growing things. This reminds you that you are connected to everything and keeps you grounded in your healing, sensual nature. You honor the Moon by creating a space that is beautiful yet utilitarian.

Keeping clutter down to a minimum may be something of a challenge for you, because you can be a bit of a packrat. Developing a routine of straightening up the house can help you feel more control in the rest of your life. Fresh cut flowers from your garden, a window planter with often-used kitchen herbs, and a medicine cabinet stocked with essential oils and replenishing lotions – these things add a touch of loveliness to the ordinary tasks of living.

In addition to the sensual, a Taurus Moon needs the practical. You may love creating delicious meals for loved ones. You feel secure when your cupboards are well stocked – especially with the foods that comfort you. Planning ahead by growing your own food, buying in bulk or saving money lets you feel that there are options in times of challenge.

Owning property or having another kind of long-term relationship with a piece of land may also support you in developing the inner security you crave. But with this Moon it is essential that you learn to find it within as well, and to look beyond the material comforts you so often rely on. Accumulating too much stuff is a pitfall for the Moon in Taurus.

Practices that remind you of the interconnectedness of all life and instill within you a sense of gratitude will keep you from falling into the trap of over-consumption. Whether it's organizing a gardening project, learning how to care for animals or singing songs with friends, when you let yourself expand into another, you gain insight into the true meaning of security.

Relationships and the Art of Loving: Defining Self-worth

With the Moon in Taurus, a desire for stability colored early childhood experiences. The Mother or caregivers of a Taurus Moon child may have made safety and security a priority. As a child, you may have experienced this as feeling controlled at all times.

These issues of control and security could have manifested as caregivers working too much and not spending enough time with you at home; reminding you of "how good you have it" if you tried to express disappointment or anxiety; or masking their own intense feelings with food addictions, over-accumulation, bad relationships or various other ways to "numb out."

If the mother-figure was able to express herself in a more conscious way, this lesson taught you that real security comes from within and that working hard to express your core values in practical, seeable ways – walking your talk – manifests true abundance.

This legacy can help a Taurus Moon understand how to provide stability for the people you love. As an adult, your inner self may focus on building healthy emotional structures that allow partners, children or friends to feel comfortable sharing their feelings. Like the abundant Mother Earth, you want to be seen as a benevolent provider who works for the good of the community.

But working that hard to maintain a sense of continual peace and prosperity can block you from your true feelings, creating long-lasting resentment or emotional grudges. To create real security in your relationships you must work toward a spirit of openness and cooperation, letting others in and collaborating more to see how love flourishes even as it changes.

You thrive when affection is shown physically and can help others feel grounded in their bodies through such demonstrations. You need frequent touch, with hugs and massages as well as an active and loving sex life. Sex for you can be a long, sweet road to pleasure, a ritual of cherishing and celebrating life. You must be careful not to let an over-reliance on routine get in the way of these physical needs. When you take the time to make love and appreciate your sensual nature, productivity in other areas of life will also soar.

The key to your art of loving is separating self-worth from externalities and asking for help when you need it. When you feed yourself love, actions can come from a place of inner peace rather than out of a motivation to be loved. The need to feel secure leads many a Moon in Taurus to stay in stagnant, unfulfilling relationships. But real security does not mean walling up the borders and maintaining order at all costs.

The systems of Earth rely on openness and an ability to respond to changing conditions to sustain such a wealth of life. A Taurus Moon's own natural sensuality can point you to the things that make you happy to be alive so that you can share such joy with others.

The Dark Side of the Moon: Hooked on a Feeling

One danger with the Moon in Taurus is to over-indulge. Endurance, something Taurus is known for, can be both a blessing and a curse. Here, the Moon gets trapped by its own need for security, and you can become locked into patterns and habits which no longer serve you but endure because they made you feel good in the past. An uncertain future breeds anxiety for the Moon in Taurus, so you may try anything to maintain control over your feelings, relationships and home. This Moon needs to learn how to go with the flow more, not getting overly attached to good feelings or helplessly stuck in bad moods.

You have a tremendous need to be appreciated and seen as valuable by your family or community, whether that value is your physical attractiveness, your gardening skills, or your way with a hammer. When you aren't getting the attention you crave, you can plummet into a dangerous cycle of seeking sensual gratification with food, sex or whatever makes you feel good.

The lesson here is to see how valuable you are without relying on external validation. When you honor your Moon, you can see the natural ebb and flow of life and understand that your own feelings travel this same cycle of ups and downs. You may always fall into ruts, but there are regular activities that can pull you out. Spending time in nature, building something with your hands or hanging out with animals can be food for your soul.

Whatever aspirations you carry within you, they will only get off the ground with practical, loving attention to your physical and emotional needs. You need to focus on the fundamentals of living on Earth: food, shelter, health, and relationships.

To step out of the darkness and into the light, you have to learn how to be present in your body rather than neglecting it, over-extending it, or trying to control it at all costs.

This Moon wants to welcome you back to your place within the circle of life, honoring all the beings that you share the planet with. When you accept your own sensual nature and the power you possess to create security from within, you will discover a happiness that is truly sustainable.

The Goddess Within: Hathor

Hathor is an ancient Goddess worshipped by the Egyptians for thousands of years. As the winged cow of creation, she created the human body to house the eternal spirit, so that we could experience pleasure and the senses. Hathor was life itself, the cycles of the seasons, ruling over the entire wheel of the human lifespan. She was present at each child's birth but also witnessed the moment of death.

She speaks:

"I give you this body, this earth, this body. All life is sustained and regulated by me. The floods, fires and famines as well as the feasts, the quiet rains and the gentle breeze. The flourishing of all life is dancing with change. Within me are rhythms, cycles and eras vaster than you can imagine. Within me, also the rhythm of the breath, the cycle of the moon, and the turning of the seasons. Earth, air, fire, water. You will befriend the elements through your senses.

"I will teach you to follow your own cycles without holding back and without shame. I will show you how to stabilize without force. I will show you that nothing is isolated, that everything is connected as a strand on the web of life, which reverberates with healthy power every time you listen to your body with loving awareness. In music and laughter, the scent of lavender, the kiss of the breeze, the taste of ripe cherries, the touch of your lover. You will find me there."

EXPLORATION

To find out more about the power of the goddess within you, explore these suggestions and questions:

When do you feel the most secure and connected?

Where are you addicted to pleasure, or to pain?

How do you seek to maintain control in your life?

What are the things that make you feel beautiful?

Moon in Gemini

♊

- Your Natural Resource: Curiosity
- Your Art of Loving: Patient communication
- The Dark Side of the Moon: Mind over matter
- The Goddess Within: Minerva

With your Moon in Gemini, you are the traveler who walks over shifting sands with no map but your own curiosity. You want excitement and feel most secure when you have ample choices. Feeling limited in any way can stifle your natural resources of curiosity and dexterity. This aptitude to make sense of things applies not only to your quick mind, but to your hands and body as well, giving you a knack for multi-tasking. You can juggle a variety of interests and ideas simultaneously. This can lead people to label you as unreliable or lacking commitment, but really you just want to learn everything you can about life. New people, places and ideas satisfy your yearning for adventure. Feeding your moon means engaging in mentally and physically stimulating activities. Your reservoir of power springs forth from this curious exploration, which in turn makes you feel connected to others.

Gemini is ruled by the planet Mercury. In classic myths, Mercury is the god of communication, crafts, traveling and storytelling. He often gets himself into trouble with his insatiable curiosity, but he just as easily gets himself out of it with his gift of language. With your Moon here, you too may get into trouble with your incessant questions, wild tales or changeable nature. You are so friendly, though, that people can quickly forgive your innocent social blunders.

Even though the Moon is personal and sometimes private, you are a social creature by nature. This Moon gives you the ability to navigate diverse and complex situations with finesse. You want to understand your world in order to fit in. Being armed with as much knowledge as possible helps you feel secure, so that you know that whatever the situation you find yourself in, you will have the dexterity to navigate the conversation and therefore be accepted by that social group.

If you find yourself in situations where you feel mentally deficient, you may resort to making it up or playing the trickster with tall tales and jokes that trip others up. Asking questions is another tactic you use to help create an "in" with someone else.

To create a home that supports a feeling of inner security, you will need to have plenty of stimulation. Shelves filled with interesting books and colorful magazines can keep you energized during downtime at home, and you probably wouldn't go anywhere without a tablet, smartphone or e-reader. You may want to set up a "control center" that plugs you into the world even when you are alone. A variety of media sources are necessary home accessories to the Gemini Moon looking to fulfill that urge toward connection. Your inner nature is best served with projects that you can easily and quickly accomplish on your own. So watch out for complicated home improvement schemes or garden plans. Just keep it simple.

In the garden, perennial flowering shrubs that don't require a lot of care add color to your life. Inside, pictures of your travels and the people you love make your walls a window to the world in a friendly, personal way. Making space in your home for friends to hang out is vital, as you love to have people around. You may want to turn one room into a workshop or craft studio so you can always have a place for the inevitable collection of projects you are juggling without cluttering up the rest of your house.

Relationships and the Art of Loving:
Patient Communication

The mother or primary caregiver of someone with a Gemini Moon is often seen as social, talkative and maybe a bit of a know-it-all. She may have been a natural storyteller, but the shadow side of this mother could have darkened her communication with outright lies and scattered attention, creating confusion and insecurity in a child who possessed a natural sensitivity to what was really going on. If this was the case, you could have developed mistrust of others and doubt in your own abilities to draw correct conclusions about the world.

These early childhood experiences and perceptions of mother imparted you with the skill to nurture and inspire others with your words. Your emotional inheritance from this Mother Moon includes an active mind and imagination that is able to instinctively respond to a variety of needs and situations with grace. You know that it's hard to be certain about anything, and for this reason you allow the people in your life a lot of leeway. You love to be surprised and kept on your toes. And yet you also need to feel that you can trust your partners and loved ones to understand you when the chips are down. To you, the most painful experience is not being able to communicate clearly with others or to have your needs misunderstood. If you find yourself with friends and lovers who just won't listen, you might need to reevaluate their presence in your life.

Because you don't want to be pinned down, your partners and friends may believe that you aren't committed to the relationship. What you really want is the relationship to stay vital and alive. For this to be possible requires honest communication with your loved ones about what you are feeling and allowing plenty of time for them to understand. These heart-to-hearts must be followed up with seeable changes in personal dynamics so you can feel certain you were understood. The practice of Active Listening is a vital tool for the Gemini Moon to have in their relationship toolbox.

The key to your art of loving is to learn patience. You need to be able to talk through emotional challenges, and you need to be honest enough with yourself to know that you're even having a feeling in the first place. Cultivating patience for you means following through on your feelings by sharing the important ones with the people you love and by admitting that you don't have all the answers. At least not yet. Let yourself be curious about what's happening inside of you. When you express your emotions to others you can find out where they're coming from, too. Allowing the outside world to meet the real you makes it truly possible for you to adjust to changes.

The Dark Side of the Moon: Mind over Matter

The Moon in an Air sign exemplifies a common conundrum in modern civilization: the split between Mind and Body. We still tend to place an overemphasis on the intellect instead of the instinct. Your body often plays second fiddle to your mind, either out of carelessness or outright intentional neglect. You are constantly on the go and easily forget to take care of yourself. Taking a breather is all your body gets when really it wants a good, long conversation (with yourself). While it is true that your naturally active lifestyle feeds your Moon the energy it craves, you are also learning that being connected doesn't mean subjecting yourself to a constant bombardment of information. Your own body is a wealth of information and is what makes all those juicy thoughts and adventures possible. Because you love to draw conclusions from what you witness, you may fall into a habit of assuming you already know something. For your changing body and emotions, this often leads to disaster in the form of recurring health problems and more often depression. For a Gemini Moon, focused breathing exercises may help you reconnect to your body and release any built-up tension.

You tend to over-intellectualize your emotions, which further disconnects you from your body. When you feel sadness, for example, you might launch into something external to take your mind off of it. Or you may instantly jump to figuring it out rather than feeling it fully. You might do some research, gaining as much information as possible on "sadness" but never really listening to your own heart.

You can also rely too much on other people to show you how you feel. For a Gemini Moon, the world reflects back to you who you are, and as a consequence you can become a kind of voyeur who lives in other people's lives but never fully inhabits your own world. To step out of the darkness and into the light, learn to reconnect to the body and value it as a reliable source of information. When you do this, you help all of us engage in new forms of holistic communication.

The Goddess Within: Minerva

Minerva is the name given to the Roman Goddess of Wisdom, known to the Greeks as Athena. Like most powerful goddess figures, her roots spread deep and wide into the soil of human story. Her name comes from the ancient word for *mind* and she ruled over all intellectual matters, as well as crafts, artisans, poetry and medicine. One of the most famous stories of Minerva is her weaving contest with the mortal Arachne, who assumed she knew everything about the art and refused to honor Minerva as the Goddess of Weaving. Arachne's weaving was indeed the best, but her pride and trickster-nature eventually gets her turned into a spider, the eternally weaving arachnid.

She speaks:

"As a child of Minerva, you can access an infinite body of wisdom and natural ability. But you must be able to recognize the source and honor the roots of such talent. Who is the Self behind your thoughts? Who are you when reason is stripped away? Thoughts, stories and ideas hold the power of intention. But you must be careful not to let them control and manipulate your essence. Your mind, like the Moon, changes in phases. Your essence is deeper and vaster than you can imagine.

"What's real? What's true? What's pure fantasy? Understand your own mind, and you will know that in complexity is beauty. Like a many faceted jewel, wisdom shines into the mind from many angles. The truly wise soul knows that the essence of creation and thought rests in emotion, matter, spirit and motion. Just as the Moon circles the Earth, your mind can be a key that opens you to love, change and growth."

EXPLORATION

As you seek out those places where you can ask questions and meet people with different ideas, you will empower your own inner nature, which is deliciously complex and beautifully stimulating. Satisfy your inquisitiveness and mental dexterity by volunteering at the local radio station, taking classes at a community school, or joining a group that meets regularly for activities like sightseeing, current events discussions, or arts and crafts. Remember to breathe.

To find out more about the power of the goddess within you, explore these suggestions and questions:

Are your relationships too complex, or do they rely too heavily on simple, safe assumptions?

What do you think about your body?

How do you seek security through knowledge?

Where does uncertainty live in your life?

How do you rely on others to form your beliefs?

Moon in Cancer

- Your Natural Resource: Cycles of feeling
- Your Art of Loving: Born to love
- The Dark Side of the Moon: The moody blues
- The Goddess Within: Yemaya

The Moon is quite at home in its ruling sign of Cancer. This placement gives you a natural ability to flow with your emotions and offer nurturing to yourself and others. Your reservoir of power includes an innate understanding of the cycles that flow through everything – people, oceans, plants. When you allow yourself to truly ride the tides of your changing inner life, you are able to make more positive impacts on the world around you. You feel really good when you can take care of others and provide them with what they need to flourish. And you trust that those you care for will in turn feed you energy and love in a natural exchange. It is this ebb and flow, like the cycle of the moon and the tides of the ocean – that rules the heart of a Cancer Moon.

The Moon directs the pull of the ocean, creating the tides that create a rich diversity of aquatic life and are thought to have helped create the circumstances needed for life to begin in the first place.* This amazing, life-giving lunar energy is your inner power as well, directing you to create and tend to the emotional wellness and health of those you love.

When Earth's oceans face environmental dangers, the threat extends beyond the shoreline. Similarly, when your own emotions are out of whack, you may look for ways to offer support and healing to others. This is because you are so emotionally connected to them, you feel that taking care of others will help you feel better, too. When you sense that others feel healthy and cared for, you feel healthier. When you are in your power, you can give and receive love easily, like the ebb and flow of the tides. However, when your shadow is strong, your ebb and flow becomes more like a tug of war. You can create expectations that others act happy so you can feel better about yourself. Enforcing emotional contentment wrings all the joy out of giving and receiving.

Cancer rules the home, family and emotions, so you probably pay a great deal of attention to these matters. Having a home that provides you and your loved ones with a sense of belonging is vital. For a Cancer Moon, home is where the heart is. Family dinners and other group activities that bring your loved ones together help keep the wheels turning for you. Striving to carve out a comfortable nest for yourself will awaken your natural rhythms. As the symbol of Cancer, the crab is a beautiful metaphor as well as a challenge to consider as you create your ideal home. The crab has an outer shell of protection, a vital necessity to shield its soft and vulnerable body underneath. Your home provides you with just such a layer of protection.

More so than most other Moon signs, you are so sensitive and tuned in to emotional states that you need a place that lets you feel safe. Your home can give you a nourishing respite from the rest of your life. Soft lighting and cushy chairs, special cases for family heirlooms and keepsakes, a kitchen amenable to frequent home-cooked meals – these are just some ideas of how you might make your home a shelter of love and protection. Your home can easily become packed with objects because you are reluctant to part with anything that has a fond memory attached to it. Your garden will help you access your inner power by filling it with a variety of herbs and vegetables that can nourish and heal your family and friends. The challenge implicit within the symbol of the crab is to not close yourself off completely to the rest of the world like a crab withdrawing into its shell. You are here to offer nourishment and emotional healing to yourself and your family. Making your home a calm place where you can replenish your soul and receive support from other people will help you feel more confident out in the world.

Relationships and the Art of Loving: Born to Love

With this placement, it may have seemed as though your mother or other primary caregiver was born to be a mom. She may have instilled in you the importance of family, showing you how to honor your roots and taking the time to build strong bonds between living relatives. Because this Moon has an intense desire to belong, situations in early childhood may have demanded that personal desires be subordinated to the wellbeing of the family unit. You may feel that your mother gave up her own identity in the pursuit of family security. But part of this Moon's identity is in fact realized through acts that provide safety for the family.

Your emotional inheritance grounds you in these traditional family values, and you can use this foundation to create structures that in turn foster strong bonds between you and your loved ones. You are a natural at sensing what others need to feel supported and loved. The blurred line between yourself and others is both a blessing and a challenge. You can naturally blend into emotional states and situations in order to stabilize the environment. This makes you feel more secure and makes others feel appreciated and understood. But if you bleed too much into another's reality, you may feel cheated out of your own authentic experience, eventually becoming resentful of the very people you are trying hard to nurture. And they may become distant in an effort to separate from you. When you feel centered within yourself, you can intuitively recognize how others are feeling. When you block your own emotions and let your insecurities guide you, your clarity is diminished along with your ability to nurture others.

The key to your art of loving is finding ways to authentically express your own needs without bending too far to accommodate other people. Because you feel more at ease when you sense that others are comfortable, you may not notice parts of yourself that are still hungry for love. Tapping into your inner power gives you insight and compassion for natural cycles. Sometimes you feel content and other times uncertain and afraid. Understanding this, you can learn to take more room for your own needs, knowing that as in all things, there is an ebb and flow. Your emotions may be a rhythmic tide of changes, but your love endures.

The Dark Side of the Moon: the Moody Blues

When your Moon in Cancer takes a dive into the dark waters, you come face to face with your own issues of control and self-doubt. Because you desire security in the form of a nurturing, loving home life, you sometimes suppress the natural cycle of upsets and strains found in every relationship. You want the people you love to be free of suffering and sorrow, but sometimes you take this wish to the point of stifling others' healthy emotional expression. This can take shape in a number of common ways, such as offering food to someone who's down in the dumps. You might think you are expressing love and support through such actions, but you are actually sending an unconscious message to "shut up." It could be that this is the way emotions were dealt with in your own childhood.

Whenever you find yourself feeling insecure, impatient or unavailable for other people, it may be a clear signal that you have your own unexpressed feelings to attend to. The Moon in Cancer has a reputation as being moody and irrational. Such dismissive attitudes toward people who feel deeply can be attributed to widespread cultural conditioning that encourages us to regularly disconnect from our emotions. But the responsibility to listen to your mood swings and tempers rests squarely with you. When you are acting irrational and like a *lunatic*, it might be because a vital need is being ignored either by you, within your family, or even in the larger community. If you continue to ignore the warning signs, you may later find yourself cleaning up the wreckage of an emotional hurricane.

When you feel vulnerable and exposed, you start on a slippery slide of self-doubt that may lead you to make wrong assumptions about loved ones. You can easily let your fears drive you, thinking that other people are deliberately trying to hurt you. The fear of being alone, of losing someone you care about or of being ridiculed or "outed" in some way can cause a cycle of feelings that feel real enough but are not based in actual circumstances. The skill of knowing when your feelings are running you and when you are running your feelings can be honed through spiritual practices such as Insight Meditation or regular "breath scans" that put you in touch with what you're really feeling in the moment.**

To step out of the darkness and into the light, it is important that you learn to lightly touch the surface of your emotions, allowing them full expression without going so deep that you end up drowning. You can easily manifest illness, especially as stomach problems, in the breasts or chest area, or even as tumors

– all of which are ruled by the sign of Cancer. The waves of your emotional cycles may be subtle or they may be tempests. Letting them through will help release you from bondage to fear and insecurity. You are a sensitive, intuitive, nurturing person. Don't let anyone try to tell you these qualities are unimportant. They are imperative at this time in our human history, and the more you listen to and flow with your emotions, the more healing you can create in the form of open, loving, conscious families. Everyone needs to be loved and to be told they are loved. You are a gateway that opens to more authentic, emotional self-expression.

The Goddess Within: Yemaya

The Goddess Yemaya comes from the Yoruba tradition of West Africa. Yemaya is a Moon Goddess but is primarily associated with the seas. She rules the surface of the ocean, as opposed to the watery depths. Close to the surface the ocean teems with a diversity of life forms, and Yemaya is a Mother Goddess, a protectress and nurturer of life.

She speaks:

"My darling child, I want you to know that I love you. I want you to know that no matter what you feel, I love you. I want you to feel the truth of my love. No matter what you do, I love you still. You are worthy of love merely by being; it is your birthright to love, to be loved, to be love.

"My own presence is calming and cleansing, for I am the breath of life itself, and the womb of all creation. When these waters are stirred by deep feelings or real threats, storms may rage over my open seas. I allow this upheaval, and even in the storms I calmly ride its waves to the other side. For in the power of my storms is the power to heal. In the frightful power of destruction, I can cleanse myself of impurity and become centered again. In knowing my own cycles, I show you how to be at peace with whatever the winds of change may blow your way."

EXPLORATION

You may want to experiment with keeping track of the Moon and how the cycle of the Moon affects you. You can also implement regular emotional check-ins with your loved ones in an effort to keep the channels open for all phases of feeling.

To find out more about the power of the goddess within you, explore these questions:

How do you nurture others in your life?

In times of trouble, what do you do to take care of yourself?

What makes you feel like you are not worthy of love?

How does the past have a hold on you?

In your desire to merge with others, do you forsake your own emotional needs?

*Bruce Lieberman, paleobiologist at the University of Kansas in Lawrence says, "I suspect that eventually life would have made land without the tides. But the lineages that ultimately gave rise to humans were at first intertidal." Quoted from *Without the Moon, Would There Be Life on Earth?* by Bruce Dorminey, *Scientific American*, April 21, 2009.

**Practices like meditation and breath scans help focus one's attention on the present moment and see what's going emotionally, mentally and physically. To find more exercises, go to: http://joannamacy.net/engaged-buddhism/spiritual-practices-for-activists.html.

Moon in Leo

♌

- Your Natural Resource: Enthusiasm
- Your Art of Loving: A playful heart
- The Dark Side of the Moon: Me, me, me
- The Goddess Within: Bast

With your Moon in Leo, you have a sense of the dramatic. Your reservoir of power is chock-full of glamour and enthusiasm. Talent and creativity come naturally to you, and that inner resource of sunlight helps you step into leadership roles. When your Moon is blocked, it may seem that your life is one big tragedy and that all your energy must go into overcoming obstacles rather than creating works of art. But being in touch with your emotions can be an inspiration. The trick is to not get so caught up in your own drama that your life becomes the work of art. Instead ride your feelings to the nearest outlet – writing, painting, dancing, singing, ritual making. When you take the time to express yourself in these ways, you'll have the extra energy to channel attention to a healthy career, relationship or home.

Shakespeare's famous line that "all the world's a stage" is your personal mantra and your home needs to carry this energy for you. This means letting yourself indulge in home designs that speak to your playful and artistic side. Your flair for the romantic may want to create a luscious, richly colored and textured bedroom. Your flair for style may make your closet resemble a costume store or boutique. And the mirrors – ah well, let's just say they are your favorite home accessory. Don't shy away from it. Lean into self-love to create a home that feels comparable to your own gregarious personality. Just be mindful of the bills, darling, as your extravagant side can get you into financial trouble.

Your Moon in Leo wants a steady supply of art and beauty to surround you, but that could just as easily be interesting people instead of lush, expensive furniture. So make sure you create an atmosphere that's conducive to entertaining others, for you love a party. When you feel that your home is indeed the stage upon which you can fully and freely express your whole self without shame, guilt or insecurity, then you will be better able to offer your fiery flair to the rest of the world.

Your reservoir of power can offer a surge of healing to others by providing them with an example of how to be themselves and follow their hearts. When you are expressing your natural enthusiasm, you can more easily be filled with acceptance and joy in the joy of others, rather than struggling with notions that there isn't enough recognition to go around.

Relationships and the Art of Loving: Playing by Heart

With your Moon in Leo, you may have experienced a bit of glamour around your mother or other primary caregiver. Life may have been a party whenever she entered the room. On the other hand, a Leo Moon can indicate a mother who never grew up. The shadow side of this Mother Moon tends toward arrogance and melodrama. It may be that you had to vie for attention and love. Whatever the case, early childhood experiences made you crave big life and big love, giving you a glimpse of the ways you might tap into your own inner resource and unleash the lion within.

Throughout your childhood, you may have learned that the way to get love was by expressing yourself, whether that meant grabbing the spotlight or joyfully sharing your ideas with others. This rich and fiery emotional inheritance provides you with the tools to encourage others to be whoever they are and open up to their own dramatic sides. You are incredibly affectionate and can be loyal to a fault. You want everyone to feel special and to create relationships full of romance and play. Your own instincts for flair help the people in your life tap into greater joy and celebrate the artistry inherent in all walks of life.

Early childhood patterns may have created a need within you to experience relationships as exciting and dramatic. This can lead you to balk at commitment once the initial thrill is gone. "Falling in love" is often more appealing than being in a relationship. A sense of boredom may lead you to outrageous behaviors. Playing the field is one thing, but there's another word for that these days: *player*. Sometimes, your need to feel special manifests as the attention-seeker who steals everyone's thunder and makes others feel unimportant except as admirers or attendants to the queen/king. Be mindful of behavior that one-ups what someone is expressing to you. "Oh, you're afraid of spiders? Well, I am so afraid of them, that once I crashed my car into a building because one was crawling on my leg." That sort of thing.

The other side of this golden coin is your inherent generosity and great big lion heart. The key to your art of loving is emitting the radiance of the Sun, which comes naturally through you when you allow for others to be special in their own ways. Giving yourself time for artistic exploration and play is essential to feeding your moon. Everyone in your life will be much happier if you are being creative. When you try to hide your light under a bushel, you end up resenting the people you're trying to protect from your fire. When you demand that others bow down to your glory, you miss out on the joy of giving someone else the chance to shine. Trust that by giving in to your creative side and cultivating your natural enthusiasm for love, others will see the real you and appreciate the flair you bring into their lives.

The Dark Side of the Moon: Me, Me, Me

Leo is naturally ruled by the Sun, which is the symbol of the Self and our conscious action. But the Moon is all about the collective and our instinctual nature. You may feel that in order to belong (Moon), you have to prove that you are special (Sun). Or maybe you feel that you are automatically entitled to special treatment, because you already know that you are, in fact, dazzling. Whatever the case, you have a strong need for constant affection or adoration, and this sets the stage for movie-sized circumstances to erupt if other people's attention begins to wane. Rather than subconsciously fanning the flames of your lion-sized ego, recognize when you're making things up.

Because you are a natural actor, you can feel things that aren't actually true for you but that serve your need to get noticed. You take things hard and can blow up a small irritation into an apocalypse. Needing the spotlight in relationships is not in itself shameful. But when you go to the dark side, you create drama and stir up the emotional energy needlessly. Such a moment of lapsed emotional integrity can upset even the healthiest of relationships. Instead of resorting to such heavy-handed theatrics, consider the types of romantic gestures that make you feel special and let your partner know about them.

Leos are often criticized for excessive pride and bravado, but they are actually incredibly sensitive to others' opinions. This is especially true with the Moon in Leo. Someone at work doesn't like your idea, or a lover makes a careless remark, and you fall to pieces. Even though it may have been a small rebuke, the feeling behind the puffed-up pout is real enough. Just because you appear confident and willing to take risks, doesn't mean you like making mistakes. Another's negative response makes you feel as though you failed. Learning to release painful emotions through bodywork, art, or ritual can help you re-establish that intuitive connection. Summon up that Leo courage and ask your friends for reflection on confusing situations. The good news is that even though you are quick to feel the wound, you bounce back just as fast with the love and support of good friends.

Stepping out of the darkness and into the light means approaching the emotional realm of relationships with playfulness and courageous self-expression. You understand that being a "child of the Sun," gives you the freedom to trust your instincts to lead you in the right direction. The more you feel that love is unconditional, the more authentic you can be in responding to situations that require a bit of tact along with your fiery Leo Moon enthusiasm.

The Goddess Within: Bast

Bast, or Bastet as she is sometimes known, was revered by the Egyptians as a solar deity, but her feline form associates her with the moon as well. Throughout her long worship, she has been called the Goddess of pleasure, war, cats, music and dance, and motherhood. In all things, her devotion and ferocity are revered. Her festivals were said to be completely wild and raucous affairs but had serious intentions to generate healing, protection and fertility.

She speaks:

"The priestesses in my temples danced for the joy of it. They let pleasure guide them, in sex and celebration, drama and bawdy laughter. Their hearts were open so they had nothing to hide. They gave freely and yet were themselves free from obligation. No duty but to the beating heart and the flame of inspiration.

"I am that flame. I am the fire of the radiant sun, sent forth in the morning to illuminate each part of you. If you know me, you become the child who lives in trust and the protector of your own heart. You don't have to know what's going on when the beautiful complexity of life draws you into its wise and silly games. Trust me, and the flames of creation fall from your fingertips. Open to me, and we will dance with wild abandon. Desire me, and the beauty you seek will explode from within you."

EXPLORATION

The Moon in Leo invites you to appreciate your flair for drama, your fiery heart and your passion for life. Engaging in activities that invite creativity and playfulness into your day-to-day life will help you to feel more connected to your essence. All pop psychology aside, you really need to let that inner child have a say in your life.

To find out more about the power of the goddess within you, explore these questions:

What are the ways that you know you are special?

Do you know how to play and take yourself less seriously?

How do you express yourself both artistically and emotionally?

Where do your creative juices want to flow?

How do you make space for the people you love to shine?

Moon in Virgo

- Your Natural Resource: Mindfulness
- Your Art of Loving: The perfect question
- The Dark Side of the Moon: The quest for perfection
- The Goddess Within: Ishtar

Virgo, symbolized by the virgin, is ruled by the planet Mercury, who here symbolizes intelligence, thoroughness and order. In Virgo, we ask ourselves: *How do we organize the information we've gathered?* We've engaged in self-discovery and exploration; now, what do we do with it? What stays and what goes?

With your Moon in Virgo, you are naturally gifted in the skill of discernment, and this springs from your inner power of mindfulness toward all you do. You want to know all the parts of yourself, to tabulate the skills you bring, and to sharpen up your résumé so you can get to work. With your Moon grounded in Virgo's domain, you analyze past experiences and behavior, looking for ways to improve and perfect your role in the world. It's true that you want to feel useful and not waste your time in fruitless efforts. While this highlights the practical side of Virgo, the Moon calls forth your pure heartfelt devotion to serve and heal suffering.

The Moon in Earth signs needs physical touch and affection in order to feel emotionally secure. Virgo is not usually attributed an overly sensual nature, but you are more effective and powerful when you are being fed with reassuring, healing touch. Your inner resource of mindfulness builds from paying attention to and valuing your own body. Overcoming any shame or undervaluing of your body will ground you into the real source of your power. For you, the sacred is alive in the regular daily actions you take to maintain your body, your family, your home and your job. What you eat, how you energize and exercise your body, the work that you do – any seemingly routine activity can become the spiritual sustenance that feeds your Moon and reconnects you to the broader aspirations you carry within.

To awaken and honor this power of mindful attention, you will want a home that is uncomplicated, one that supports you in creating rituals of magic as you cook, clean and garden your way to wholeness. Once you understand the ways your domestic side wants expression, your home will become a place of clarity and calm. You have a natural sense of organization, which may manifest as a strong need to keep things tidy. But what you're really after is a safe and orderly place where you can take stock of things before taking the next step.

To function at your peak, it's important for you to continually shed what's unnecessary, refining the gadgets and products that keep your kitchen, bathroom and garden going. It's just as important not to get carried away with a never-ending search for perfection that keeps you from noticing how great your home already is. This is a classic undervaluing trait of a Moon in Virgo. Your practical side will keep excess spending at bay, but it's the emotional debt you rack up that can hurt your dreams of building a sensible and peaceful home life. Focusing on what makes you feel good physically will always lead you to the right solutions. Your garden will flourish with native edibles and herbs that you can turn into healthy food and home remedies. The places of vital importance to you are your kitchen and your desk, because it is from these places that you can contemplate and implement the small steps that lead you to inner wellness and help you to support the people you love.

Relationships and the Art of Loving: The Perfect Question

With your Moon in Virgo, you may be constantly evaluating your early relationship with your Mother or other primary caregiver, looking for clues to your own personality. In your mind's eye, she may have been either the perfect provider or the dispenser of judgment. She could make you the most nourishing food, take you on long walks and help you with your studies; or she could make you feel inadequate, take away your dreams and admonish you to "get real." Most likely she fell somewhere between these two extremes. As a child, you could have taken in more than your fair share of self-critical, negative thinking. The point is not to figure out exactly how to measure up to the mom figure in your life, or to spend the rest of your life running screaming in the other direction. With this Moon, it's a matter of honestly asking yourself what you needed as a child and listening for the answer. There were triumphs and failures, some good things and some bad. This lunar lesson is a lot about how to take in the useful information without hyper-analysis or harsh judgment.

These childhood experiences may have left you feeling a little shy and reserved, because you want to be certain before you commit. You have a streak of sovereignty in your Moon as well as that tendency to be hypercritical, so living with others creates its share of snags as you learn how to navigate someone else's routines and habits. But you can utilize your gifts of communication and organization in order to implement an agreeable compromise. Because you root out what's inessential, you often find that people actually have similar desires and intentions even if their methods differ.

Your naturally mindful demeanor makes you a helpful partner and friend. You have the potential to offer great healing in your relationships, giving the perfect advice or suggestions whenever someone is in need. You often intuitively know when someone's in need, and like a good ER doctor, you are ready to jump into action and stay there until the last wound is stitched up. It's important to remember, though, that sometimes people want to figure things out on their own, so be sure your loved one wants your help before you offer it. Because you are so tuned in to what's happening, you can easily discern the right action that will bring about meaningful change. But when someone is feeling less than adequate, your help may come off as criticism and judgment. Utilize your mindfulness to read the emotional layout as well as the physical or practical situation. You may find that what your friends and partners need most is your loving presence rather than your calculated analysis. Let them ask for your opinion if you sense they are in an emotionally vulnerable space.

The key to your art of loving is being attuned enough to the present moment to be able to ask the perfect question. A question admits that you don't have all the answers, and it puts you in touch with the other person's experience in a way that ignites your compassion. When you trust that others are capable and strong, you can release self-defeating judgments and fears that lock you away from relationships.

The Dark Side of the Moon: The Quest for Perfection

Your strong desire for perfection can lead to self-destructive behaviors. You can be incredibly hard on yourself, expecting 110% in everything you do. This heavy work ethic means that sometimes your own emotional, physical and mental health gets the short end of the stick. You feel that you have to be in control and therefore repress unwieldy emotions. When your true feelings go unexpressed, the Virgo Moon manifests issues with food, body and other health concerns. This means you may have specific food allergies or sensitivities that flare up during times of stress. You may even struggle with eating disorders or an obsession with exercise. You probably harbor some pretty unrealistic expectations of how your body should look. Even in spiritually engaging exercises like yoga, you may push yourself to the limits in an effort to attain perfection. Virgo rules digestion and the intestines, so pay attention if symptoms in these parts of your body emerge. It could be a signal that your sensitive Moon has some deep feelings to share.

This quest for perfection may also keep you from stepping out and offering your skills because you're waiting to be completely ready. Maybe you think you're not good enough the way you are, but Virgo learns a lot on her feet. By stepping into roles even when you aren't completely ready, you will gain practical experience that helps you feel more confident in the long run. Be careful of workaholic tendencies, another favorite Virgo addiction. Remember that by caring for your own body and mind, you create deeper energy reserves to work from.

For you, stepping out of the darkness and into the light means finding a routine of self-care that is realistic and specific to your needs. The latest diet fad will not necessarily work for you, nor will trying to fit in a trip to the gym when your schedule is already packed. Trust your own body in finding the foods that nurture you. Create opportunities to move your body that flow into other regularly scheduled activities, such as biking to work or gardening. Moon in Virgo people benefit from practices that harmonize the body-mind connection, such as yoga, tai chi or other meditation forms. Tapping into your reservoir of power means learning to be mindful of your needs. When you take time to bask in the light of your Virgo Moon, you instinctively discern the way to simpler, more fulfilling lifestyle and relationship choices.

The Goddess Within: Ishtar

On the surface, a goddess typically associated with sex, love, sacred prostitution and war may seem an unlikely pairing with a Virgo Moon. But Ishtar's story is one of self-discovery and selfless commitment to serve humanity. On her journey to the underworld to rescue her lover, Ishtar strips away the layers of her identity in order to find the essence of herself. The priestesses at her temples served as judges in disputes, as great healers, and as sacred prostitutes, initiating people into respectful relationships with their own bodies. Like the symbol of Virgo itself, she is a Virgin Goddess – the ancient meaning of which is "whole and complete unto herself."

She speaks:

"I am known throughout many lands and by many names. I am Ishtar, and no gate is closed to me. I journey to the worlds both above and below. And to my own temples, I welcome all.

"Some find me holding a lotus and mirror, reflecting the way to wisdom. Others see two snakes in my hand, and they learn the path of healing and shedding skin. Some see me riding a lioness through the sky, aiming my fiery arrows at enemy and error. Others know me as The Lover, whose devotion is unmatched, whose skills are refined in the art of love.

"In all these aspects – however you may see me – I give myself fully. I say yes to every moment and plunge in. You, my friend, are just as raw. You are mind but body too. Let yourself succumb to the pleasure of the moment, to the question that it asks of you: Can you be with me, can you be here and now with me?"

EXPLORATION

The Moon in Virgo can lead you to understand more about your essence as servant of life, as healer, as grand organizer of all things pertinent. You can get the job done, as long as you are taking time for your own body and mind to connect and communicate. Ishtar is a goddess who travels to the underworld in order to know herself more fully. It is a dangerous and excruciating journey, but the person who knows who they are can offer exactly what is needed in any situation. She can guide you to the truth and potential.

To find out more about the power of the goddess within you, explore these questions:

What are the skills and talents that you embody?

How do you honor past experiences that have helped shape you, while shedding attachments to old hurts?

What worries and doubts keep you from being mindful of the moment?

Do you know when to be the judge, when to be the healer and when to be the lover?

What helps your mind retain its natural clarity?

Moon in Libra

♎

- Your Natural Resource: Restoring harmony
- Your Art of Loving: Heartfelt communication
- The Dark Side of the Moon: Hiding out
- The Goddess Within: Persephone

Libra is ruled by the planet Venus, Goddess of Love and Beauty. With your Moon in Libra, you need beautiful surroundings in order to feel secure and may show a naturally artistic side. You crave partnership and living with others in order to feel secure, although you'd rather forgo the disagreements that cohabitation brings. Your natural resource is harmony, and this instinct to set things right brings with it the art of diplomacy. You are a charming and soft communicator who works through personal emotions and issues by dialoguing with loved ones. Silence can be excruciating for a Libra Moon if it means that someone is either not willing to listen or talk over their own feelings. You are here to run the energy of beauty and grace through you and into your relationships, home and work. When you are in your power, you have an innate sense of what is just and equitable. You move to balance things when the scales are tipped too far, and this helps restore peace to our troubled times.

People with the Moon in Libra can be especially fearful of conflict, as they revere harmony and beauty above all. With this placement, you are most likely an exceptional listener as well as a big talker. Your Moon may tell you to utilize these skills to mediate and de-escalate emotionally charged situations. But you would do well to honor the conflicts within you and accept your own contradictions as well.

Libra Moons have a luxurious and elegant aesthetic, and you will want to surround yourself with exquisite art and other beautiful objects. Your home will best serve your inner power when it is decorated with soothing colors and textures, full of soft light, and spacious enough to let your airy nature roam. You want to feel comfortable in all ways, from the food you eat, to the couch you lounge on, to the soft feather comforter on your bed. You're not necessarily a neat-freak, but you do strive to preserve harmony in your home. This means that sometimes the day-to-day clutter gets pushed under the rug or into the closet so you can just relax. Eventually, you have to face the dust hiding in the corners. The spring and autumn equinoxes are good times for you get down to the business of sorting, discarding and beautifying. It's important for you to create a space that can host social gatherings, from old-fashioned salons to friendly, informal potlucks. Spending enough time just hanging out in the easy company of good friends helps you feel emotionally connected, even if the conversation stays light. Such socializing supplies you with a sense of inner security and helps you channel your harmonizing power into work and other broader goals.

Relationships and the Art of Loving:
Heartfelt Communication

The sign of the Moon in our charts can tell us more about the relationship we have with our mothers, or other primary caregiver. With the Moon in Libra, you learned early on to balance your needs with the needs of others. As a child, you may have understood more than others exactly how much your own welfare depended upon the wellbeing of the other people in your life. To ensure that your own needs for peace and harmony were met, you may have become the diplomat in your family. Your mother or other primary caregiver could have modeled social grace, whether that meant hosting parties or just keeping the peace in your immediate family. But she may have also let go of her own ideas or suppressed her feelings in order to preserve order. This sent a message to you that strong emotion was the enemy of a calm, stable home life and should be avoided at all costs. This Mother Moon also bestows on you a rich emotional inheritance that includes an eagerness to communicate, an eye for art and a mind that instinctively sees the balance point of a situation.

Growing up, you may have learned the importance of "keeping up appearances" and being friendly, even if below the surface lurked terrible or traumatic events. You became adept at hiding troubling events from others or even from yourself in an effort to focus on the sunny side of life. When this attitude carries over into your current relationships, you can miss out on true intimacy and deep friendship. Because you strive for harmony in all things, you find beauty very easily even in challenging situations. However, you have to strive to let the light into those dark corners if you want to feel true happiness.

With your Moon in an Air sign, you need to process your feelings through the mind rather than through dramatic emotional displays. You might want to talk about your feelings instead of just feeling them. Or you may be worried that your feelings will hurt or bother other people, so you withhold expressing them entirely. For you, other people are vital to your sense of security, so you will alternately seek them out for guidance and reflection or hide away out of fear of rejection. While you do need a bit of intellectual distance from your emotions, by encouraging yourself that emotions are acceptable even when conflict arises from them, you help release yourself from the stress and strain of "being nice." Trust that your loved ones want to hear what you're feeling and make enough space in your life to let them air out their upsets.

The key to your art of loving is using your impressive skills of communication to get to the heart of matters. You may be subconsciously holding yourself and loved ones to an oppressive idea of peace, one that forces ugly and intense emotions to go into hiding. If you can instead see peace as a complicated process of deepening intimacy, you make room for a variety of emotional responses. Putting all the options on the table, even the crazy or disconcerting ones, will show you new avenues for creating a more vibrant sense of harmony than you ever thought possible.

The Dark Side of the Moon: Hiding Out

When your Moon is out of balance, it creates a sense of anxiety, manifesting a subconscious desire to eradicate any perceived flaw or shortcoming in yourself or your partner. Just like a picture slightly tilted on the wall, once you see it you will not be able to relax until it is taken care of. Your luscious aesthetic and natural sense of beauty can sometimes place too much emphasis on your own physical attractiveness as well. You can become obsessed with appearances and spend too much time and money striving to reach an ideal of what's beautiful. You may think that if you aren't charming and attractive, no one will love you. But when you suppress parts of yourself, people feel as if they don't know the real you. Instead of trying to suppress those flaws and feelings, you have to embrace them. Feelings are only moments; if we let them run through us they usually go away, leaving us with valuable information about our bodies, our needs, and our hidden gifts.

When you honor and listen to your Moon, you unlock the loving ability to understand where others are coming from and honor the differences between people. Listening to your Moon means not hiding away from painful emotions but going deeper within to feel what you feel. It's true that you need to use that elegant mind to make sense of it all, but first you have to be willing to stay present with your emotions so that they can deliver their messages.

Your Libra Moon can become so embedded in comfort-consciousness that you have a hard time taking action. It can take all of your resolve to break out of certain habits that may feel good on the surface but cause inner strife or ill health. Sometimes, it's your gift of being able to see all sides that keeps you from making a decisive move. If "it's all good," then it doesn't really matter what you do, right? But you are learning how to act in a way that's true for you, following your instincts, even if that means making the wrong decision or coming up against opposition. If a situation becomes stressful or unpleasant, you can hide out from the person causing the discord. Remember that your inner strength flows from harmony, and that means creating balance between apparent opposites. When you hide out, you are actually feeding energy to the negative emotions you wish to escape. When you summon up the courage to face situations that are stressful, you naturally uncover beautiful solutions to those nagging problems, restoring true balance to your relationships.

To step out of the dark and into the light, you must learn the art of embracing the shadow within. Like all arts, you don't master it in one day; it's a lifelong passion and practice. A Libra Moon connects you to a limitless source of power to make the world more beautiful and harmonious. But there's really only one way to do that, and it takes applying some love and attention to those less desirable parts of yourself. Healing the distressing or damaged parts of yourself instead of staying on the pleasant surface of your life opens the door to true inner harmony and makes lasting peace a little more possible for us all.

The Goddess Within: Kore-Persephone

In many ancient myths, goddesses are part of a trinity best known as Maiden-Mother-Crone. Sometimes it is hard to separate them clearly into one aspect or another. This is true of the goddess Kore-Persephone who is called Kore in her form as the young, beautiful maiden, although sometimes she is known as Persephone in both of her forms as maiden and crone, the queen of the dead. All of us have to mature from the innocence of childhood to the knowledge of adulthood. In Persephone's story, she is out picking Narcissus flowers when she is abducted and taken to the underworld. There, she becomes the wife of Hades and henceforth must spend half of the year in the Underworld and half above on the Earth. It is not an easy journey, and she must face all the disowned and ugly parts of humanity. But truly, she has to accept the unloved parts of herself as well, and acknowledge the power of the mysterious forces that move within her.

She speaks:

"I've been waiting for you down here in the dark. You knew it had to come to this. You picked the flower thinking, "oh, that's so pretty," and then the earth cracked open and swoosh, you're in hell. Well, join the club. Everyone's got demons. You can work with that. You are the most amazing juggler there is. You run energy like it was a river. Sometimes you have to breathe deep and remember that you can have peace just by choosing peace. But sometimes you have to flow underground, where the air can't reach. Here, you won't always like or understand your feelings. But you bring beauty even to the dankest quarters. Use it. Work it.

"What, are you going to just pile all your bad feelings up in the back room? Eventually, it comes cascading out into your pretty

little house, so you might as well work with it as it comes. Listen to me: when you deal with your emotions, you get to be Queen with a great steamy marriage full of passion and real love.

"Choose your journey. Are you going to walk with me, or are you going to play nice and miss out on the real thing? Life is pain, honey. Fold it into your curves and work it like a risky outfit that sets off those fierce eyes. Then you'll see that the beauty you're always trying to attain is in your darkness as well as your light."

EXPLORATION

To walk with Persephone, you have to find the courage to go into the shadow. You have to realize that there are no bad decisions. Failures are one of the most powerful ways to learn. Choose and see what happens.

To find out more about the power of the goddess within you, explore these suggestions and questions:

What are the parts of myself that I truly adore and what parts do wish I could make disappear?

How do I use beauty as a mask?

What are the qualities I see in my friends, partners, family that I admire?

In my relationships, do I run away from conflict or secretly fan the flames of discord?

How could my shortcomings and flaws be hidden treasures?

Moon in Scorpio

♏

- Your Natural Resource: Passion
- Your Art of Loving: Transformation
- The Dark Side of the Moon: Extreme behavior
- The Goddess Within: Hecate

Scorpio gets a bad rap. It's too intense, too secretive, too possessive, too unpredictable. Our society may tend to focus more on the surface of things rather than dipping into the dark, deep waters of the subconscious. But your Moon in Scorpio deserves to be treasured, for it has the vitally important work of transformation to offer to the world. Your reservoir of power is passion, whether for another person, a place, a spiritual path or self-discovery. Once you understand and open to this natural resource, you will be able to bring the energy of transformation to whatever you do in ways both healing and revealing. Feeding your Moon means honoring the Mystery. There are some essential parts of life that can't be named completely but must be explored. This requires trust as well as a willingness to try new things. Fear of the unknown, keeping secrets and obsessing about others' behavior are the obstacles to letting your passion flow freely.

It is advisable for you to make time in your life for this Mystery-seeking. This could take the form of therapy, spiritual study (especially esoteric teachings), or anything that makes you feel your innate connection to the unseen forces that shape and guide us. For many Scorpio Moons, this can mean regular sex and intimacy, for in the act of merging with another, you glimpse the Oneness you yearn for. By embracing the Mystery in your life, you will tap into your well of passion. Through your fearlessness of facing what's below the surface, you inspire others to become more of who they are.

Your home must be a place where you can be yourself completely. It is your sacred temple, where you can devote yourself to the magic of transformation. Privacy is very important to you, so whether you live alone or with others, you need to ensure that you have a place where all your veils can be stripped away without fear of interruption. Because you undergo such dramatic changes throughout your life, your home may also be under constant renovation. Even when you get sentimentally attached to objects, your desire to shed and grow makes for sudden purges of your stuff, either to the curb or to the basement where it is out of sight. Try to give yourself a balance of stability and change by having a few set furniture pieces, with beautiful, natural objects that can be moved in and out. Like an altar that varies from the new to full moon, you can create a home that manifests your moods and desires in all their myriad forms. Focus on your bedroom as a refuge for intimacy and openness. Bowls filled with water and flower petals, candles and dark colors help center you and give you a feeling of peace.

Relationships and the Art of Loving: Who are You Now?

"Who are you?" The question can simultaneously strike fear in your heart and send tingles up your spine. You want people to know already. You want connection. You want karma and fate, the idea that you have a soul-mate who doesn't need to "get to know you" because they already do. You are not afraid of secrets, your own or others', but withhold revealing yourself fully until you feel certain you can trust someone. You may even wait impatiently for them to discover the real you. If your lover is taking too long, you can sabotage the whole thing through manipulative behavior or acting out your shadow parts. This gives the Moon in Scorpio a reputation for being untrustworthy and secretive. But you are really open and fearless when it comes to plumbing the depths of your own soul, and you can't wait to find someone else who can share such true passion with you.

With the Moon in Scorpio, your experience of your mother or other primary caregiver was that of an enigma. On the surface, she may have been very caring and the two of you may have shared an intense bond. But she still could have managed to make you feel insecure about whether she really loved you. Sudden outbursts of anger or despair could have added to this feeling that there was more going on here. Scorpio is often likened to a volcano, and early childhood experiences could have felt like a cycle of dormancy and eruption. This Moon is the archetype of the Dark Mother, the goddess in story and myth who shows us what we are most afraid of in order that we may "grow up" into conscious human beings.

In your current relationships, you may struggle with trust. You know instinctively that the only constant is change. This can make you so fearful of losing affection that you choose to manipulate partners and situations in ways that make you feel more secure. The paradox is that once you let go of your need for control in relationships, you will be met with the confidence to make decisions that meet the needs of both you and your partner.

You are attracted to people who aren't afraid of the dark side of life, which means you sometimes make dangerous choices in love. But this usually only happens when you are subconsciously projecting your own shadow onto another. When you accept your need for passionate experiences and your desire to merge, you can step into love without shame or reservation. The key to your art of loving is self-knowledge. When you have learned to love your own fiery depths and dark shadows, you will be able to fully accept someone else's love with perfect trust. Of course things change, but you can learn to ride the changes without getting entangled in the net of attachment or self-deception.

The Dark Side of the Moon: Extreme Behavior

The root meaning of passion is "to suffer," and with your Moon in Scorpio you know that better than any other sign. Your passionate disposition understands that in order to really live, you have to be willing to face pain and adversity. The problem is that you may have become accustomed to equating pain with life to such a degree that you miss out on the joy and pleasure that surrounds you. When things get too easy, you may even sabotage yourself. Creating a crisis in order to grow from the challenges it presents is exhausting. You are here to practice a sort of spiritual transcendence, but not at the expense of your human body. There's a saying in certain magical traditions: "Body trumps spirit." No matter what. Even though you may sense that there's something valuable to be gleaned from your suffering or from deeply spiritual experiences, you have to take care of your physical needs first. This means learning to let go of addictions to emotional roller coasters or other mood altering substances.

When your Scorpio Moon is out of balance, it can manifest as obsession. You become preoccupied with loved ones' behavior, thinking that they are hiding something or betraying you in some way. Similarly, diet and health issues may suddenly garner all of your attention. You naturally tend to swing back and forth between extremes, which is a by-product of your pure desire to feel things very deeply. Once you have decided to merge, you require intense affection and absolute commitment in love.

For you, learning to come out of the darkness and into the light is a lifelong process of self-discovery. You will always feel drawn to your own shadows and inner demons. But you can learn to manifest love and acceptance for these places, once you accept stillness. It is imperative that you establish some kind of deep connection on the spiritual or psychological level. Reading tarot cards; studying ecstatic traditions like Sufism, Wicca or Tantric sex; meeting regularly with a psychotherapist; these activities will help you to understand more of your hidden nature and lead you to healthy, inspiring expressions of your natural power, a reservoir of passion.

The Goddess Within: Hecate

Hecate, the Greek Goddess of the crossroads, calls you to her cauldron. Hecate is the Goddess of the Dark Moon and looks after the traveler, the homeless and all those whom society has forgotten. She is the crone aspect of woman – the last stage of life when the wisdom attained from living is fully realized and respected by others. The crossroads are her domain. Often described as the place where three roads meet, it is a gateway of transformation and change. When you come to a crossroads, it is time to make offerings to Hecate, to let go of your fears and step forward with passion onto the path that calls you.

She speaks:

"Come my child, come closer and I will show you. Yes, I will show you what I am stirring in my pot. Here we have the essence of you, but to look at it – to even catch a fleeting glimpse of your

greatness – you must face your own death. You who strive for wholeness must know your shortcomings, your failures, your deep darkness. Here it swirls and dissolves all around you.

"You think it cruel, I know, for a mother to display the frailty of her child's humanity. But, oh my child, I will make you more powerful for your honesty; I will make you whole with those jagged pieces; I will fold you into my dark robes and you will find infinite love. The serpent eats her tail, and you are born again and again throughout this one life. Come to me, and be opened to the point of all possibilities. Come, and find the courage to love."

EXPLORATION

As Hecate beckons you deeper into the night, she asks for nothing less than your full commitment to total integration. She calls forth your whole self. With each step on the path of transformation, you find more courage to reveal yourself to others. Let your passion be a beacon for others rather than a smokescreen.

To find out more about the power of the goddess within you, explore these suggestions and questions:

What are the parts of yourself that you have forgotten or hidden away?

What makes you feel passionate?

How could your obsessions be maps toward wholeness?

What is your relationship with death, sex and magic?

How are you like a volcano, a phoenix or a bubbling cauldron?

Moon in Sagittarius

- Your Natural Resource: Faith
- Your Art of Loving: Free love
- The Dark Side of the Moon: Truth or dare
- The Goddess Within: Sri Lakshmi

Ah, here's our intrepid explorer, bouncing with natural optimism, ready for anything, and certain that the world will make clear his/her path. Here's the Moon in Sagittarius, giving you ample access to a deep reservoir of natural faith. With your Moon hanging out in expansive Sagittarius, you are fed by a sense of adventure. Even though this Moon might not venture too far from home, you will feel most secure if you take chances and stretch the limits of your understanding. Foreign travel to exotic cultures is one way to imbue your life with a broader understanding of the world. But you can just as easily see the exotic in your own territory – going to museums of art and culture, attending international fairs and reading accounts of travel adventures. Your Moon definitely needs ample time being in nature, so going on walks through the park, hikes on the mountain or just exploring your own backyard helps you connect back into your natural resource of faith. For in nature is abundance. When the natural systems of the Earth are being respected, there is enough for everyone. You instinctively know this and thus find your faith renewed in the calls of the wild.

The Sagittarius Moon gives you a clear intuition that guides you to opportunities both beneficial and boundary-breaking. To keep that connection open and unclouded, be sure to take time to be alone and to develop a way of communicating with the Universal Source, whether that looks like ecstatic dance, quiet prayer or philosophical study. When you open to the possibility that there is a dynamic and loving force that shapes our world, you are also opening to your own talent for making good things happen in your life. Abundance is not about having loads of material possessions, which can actually make you feel bogged down. This is wealth that comes from wisdom and experience. Your natural abundance is shaped by developing confidence in your own free spirit and the inner security you gain when you act from intuition and faith.

For your home to support you in enhancing your natural faith and optimism, it needs to be as grand as you are. Even in close quarters, you strive to create a sense of spaciousness with mirrors, windows and light colors. You will probably be attracted to unusual home furnishings that lend an aura of excitement to your everyday life. Statues from different cultures; pictures of your most recent pilgrimages; or travel magazines, religious texts and foreign language dictionaries – these are some things that can help you create a home that functions as a kind of great spiritual center. You may be attracted to having a collection of Tarot cards, runes or other forms of divination and chance in order to have a quick and easy way to check in with your intuition. Your kitchen should lend itself to international cooking experiments, with an ample selection of spices. Your garden can reflect back to your free spirit, with exotic plants and places to meditate. But beyond all the trappings of culture, what you seek in life is an essential truth that unifies all people, and this often requires you to stretch your world beyond the comforts of home through travel, education, or spiritual journeys. This wellspring of faith molds you into a student of life; you want to learn all you can about law, ethics, culture, and religion in order to create your own sense of meaning.

Relationships and the Art of Loving: Free Love

With your Moon in Sagittarius, your mother or other primary caregiver might have embodied the quintessential free spirit. You may have learned that following your own path was vital, and yet a bit at odds with the steady obligations of relationships. It's possible that you elevated your mother in your mind to a very special, almost divinely inspired human. Early examples of taking risks and not being afraid to tell the truth instilled in you a sense that life is an exciting game that serves up rewards when you follow your instincts.

As a child, you had an irrepressible spirit that wanted to explore everything around you. Following your instincts for adventure enabled you to excel at a multitude of subjects on your crash course in the study of life, and you especially wanted your larger-than-life mother to take notice. If you idealized your mother too heavily, you could have felt crushed whenever her shortcomings showed, or you could have felt an intense pressure to accomplish grandiose tasks worthy of her attention. Relationships in your adult life are colored by these early childhood experiences, making you a liberating force in others' lives. It can also cause you to push too hard or make you easily bored when others fail to live up to your inner need for continuous exploration.

Overall, you exhibit a positive energy that says to others "we can do it," and you encourage your loved ones to overcome any obstacles to their dreams and schemes. Your naturally generous nature can make people feel more confident around you. Although it may be difficult for you to imagine life with just one partner, when you do decide to stick with that special someone, you fall in love with the same ferocity with which you meet everything else in your life. Your partner may be a god or goddess in your eyes, and they may feel intense pressure to do fantastic feats in order to keep up with you.

The key to your art of loving is learning how to use your natural generosity and openness to find acceptance for different perspectives. Being a free spirit doesn't give you a license to run roughshod over other people's hearts. Life may be a game, but it has very real consequences. Because you crave freedom and act on intuition much of the time, you may neglect to take the time to check in with how others are feeling. As a consequence, the distance between you and a loved one can grow to astronomical proportions as you continue to make assumptions rather than seeking out what's really going on in someone else's life. For you, navigating the complex world of relationships is an exercise in finding the balance between loyalty to your own fiery spirit and commitment to working through the everyday challenges of relating to someone else's worldview.

The Dark Side of the Moon: Truth or Dare

When your Moon is out of balance, it can manifest as anxiety and compulsive behavior. For you, this leads to an almost brutal honesty that you aim at those you love, subconsciously seeking to cut quickly to the heart of matters. This springs from your deep desire to see the essential truth at the core of everything, and you can grow impatient with processes that are taking too long. If something feels negative, you want to move on to the next thing instead of wasting your time going further down the wrong path. So you fan the flames of discontent by confessing your "true feelings" – all the inventoried failures of the relationship. Maybe you haven't been really listening to what someone is telling you and instead hear your own ideas and assumptions humming through your head like a mantra.

When you begin to feel drained by a relationship, look within yourself to see if there are strong emotional responses that you've buried with your tendency to make lemonade out of lemons. You would do your Sag Moon a great service to fully taste the bitterness, sadness and doubt that surface from time to time, rather than just instinctively moving on. Your frankness and candor are refreshing to a world weary of being fed lines and slogans, but you have a responsibility to make sure you are responding from a centered place within you rather than a desire to get things over with.

Another potential pitfall for the Moon in Sagittarius is a predisposition toward excess. You live large and will continue to do so even when your resources are shrinking. You tend to be pretty lucky and sail through financial woes with some last-minute good fortune, but excessive spending puts a strain on relationships and creates internalized worry that often manifests as health issues. Rather than thinking you need to dampen your inherent generosity and expansiveness, try to reorient your ideas of abundance. Abundance is not just about material prosperity but about feeling you have the power to do what you want to do in life. Taking classes in spiritual and personal growth can help you find internal reserves to live well through thick and thin. Instead of expensive trips and lavish gifts, your loved ones might really be craving the gift of your time.

To move out of the darkness and into the light, recognize that you need time alone to recharge. By spending time *being* rather than *doing*, you can listen to your body, your heart and your intuition to clear away any emotional static that's blocking your natural faith and optimism. Sagittarian Moons are dynamic social creatures who can enliven any environment. But sometimes the biggest adventure lies in exploring the unknown territories of your own heart.

The Goddess Within: Sri Lakshmi

Sri Lakshmi is the Hindu Goddess of prosperity, righteousness and truth. She is often depicted seated on a lotus flower with gold coins spilling forth from her hands. In stories, she is the morning sun as well as a lunar Goddess of the Ocean. She offers boons and blessings to those who are brave in action and devoted to higher education or enlightenment. While she is often called on to invoke material prosperity, she is also the Goddess of Virtue, showing us the way to attain spiritual wealth when we move beyond the ego to see the value of good works and compassionate honesty.

She speaks:

"I am the piercing blue and the dazzling gold. You meet me in the clarity of the Blue when you use your voice to speak truth. The Gold is your will, where you act from instinct and intuition. Together, the Blue and the Gold connect you to the place where you know the Higher Truth of your most beautiful unfolding – the place where you are God or Goddess incarnate. Listen from that place of faith.

"You must ask to receive. You must tell your truth to hear truth. You must give freely to find that all you need will return to you in time and with the grace of the Goddess. My darkness is vanity, dogma and slavery. My light is beauty, change and freedom. The wheel of fortune spins round and round, and what is in the center, my love? What holds you together at your core?"

EXPLORATION

Sri Lakshmi creates beauty and true wealth whenever she appears. If you are called to work with her more, take time to reflect on what you value most in your life. Contemplate the ways you view wealth, both positively and negatively.

To find out more about the power of the goddess within you, explore these suggestions and questions:

How do you view or define abundance?

What do you do when you think you've failed?

How do you feed your quest for adventure?

What do you have faith in?

How do you connect to your source – such as god/desses, nature, philosophies or the universe – when you need to believe in yourself again?

Moon in Capricorn

♑

- Your Natural Resource: Responsibility
- Your Art of Loving: Healthy boundaries
- The Dark Side of the Moon: Control freak
- The Goddess Within: Hera

The Moon in Capricorn has a deep sense of social responsibility. Capricorn is ruled by Saturn, the planet of authority, discipline, boundaries and time. With your Moon in Capricorn, your reservoir of power is a natural responsibility that includes compassion, loyalty and patience. You have a kind of inner rulebook on what's okay and what's unacceptable, and sometimes this may be difficult for people to live up to. But this is also a Moon that wants to contribute to the greater good, and you have a strong inner determination to ensure the wellbeing of others. Your wealth of skills runs deep, and you possess an instinctive ability to meet any challenge head-on with resilience and authority. When you stand firmly in your power, you will discover an innate commitment to creating a legacy that provides care and support to others in society. In a sense, you are mother to the world, a role you do not take lightly.

With the Moon in Capricorn, you do have a taste for the finer things in life, and your home will reflect those high standards of quality. Capricorn has a reputation for being ambitious, but it's not so much about having it all as it is about having the best. You want a well-functioning, ordered home that serves as a secure base of operations for your empire. If things get too messy, you may feel self-doubt and insecurity creep in, threatening to topple everything you've worked hard to create. Your home is your castle, and you demand a great deal of control over this domain. You may even prefer solitude so that you don't have to share in decision-making. But if you do live with others, you'll need to create a space that's all your own in order to feel emotionally safe. Just clearing out even a small portion of a room and claiming it for yourself will help free you from resentment and emotional stagnation.

The Moon in Capricorn requires a certain amount of financial security in order to feel at ease enough to let your emotional guard down. Find out what that means for you, whether it's money in the bank, a sizeable stock portfolio, owning property or just being debt-free. Once you know what it is, work hard to get it. When you feel like these basic needs are being met, it will be a lot easier for you to access your inner power of responsibility, building structures that support emotional intimacy and commitment.

Relationships and the Art of Loving: Tear Down that Wall

With the Moon in Capricorn, your mother or other primary caregiver may have embodied resilience and hard work. She might have had very traditional ideas about the role of wife and mother in society, and yet she would quickly step into other roles to provide whatever was needed for the maintenance of her family. Children with this Moon placement often have to fight hard for emotional and physical affection from their mothers; material needs and discipline are offered as replacements. You might have been shielded from emotions. A steady, regulated environment was seen as the best way to offer maximum security. This sent a signal pretty early on that you have to be strong and take care of business if you want to get what you want in the world.

The legacy of this Moon is deep commitment in relationships. While you value the quality of self-reliance, you want someone to share the fruit of your labors. Whether your partner looks to you as a provider or gives you certain material or social support, you will strive for consistency in your relationship, such as following through on promises and living up to expectations. If these expectations are held too tightly, then the whole house of cards may topple when anyone drops their assigned role. Let your partners, children and friends in on what's going on within you rather than hiding it. This helps them feel more secure. Remember that your inner power is responsibility (response-ability). Listen to your loved ones and ask them what they need instead of thinking you know best. Needs change. You may think that by being productive and providing material security, you will make others happy. But when you let go of control and respond to what others are saying, you will actually gain more self-confidence in your ability to provide structures of support.

The key to your art of loving is letting your guard down every once in a while so that you can be in the moment. Listening to your body, to your emotions and to others' feelings without needing to fix it right away will give you more room to see the whole picture. Your Moon in Capricorn is a source of power that gives you dedication and commitment. Your relationships will flourish when you seek the higher ground, like the mountain-climbing goat, and align your goals with the genuine needs of your loved ones. This is the true meaning of responsibility, your natural resource.

The Dark Side of the Moon: Control freak

When your Moon is out of balance, it manifests as general anxiety and compulsive behavior. Capricorn is the sign of restriction and limitation, and with the Moon there, it can feel a bit like building a dam on a rushing river. In this case, feelings can build up behind the dam for too long, and explode in dangerous ways when they finally burst through. You may also suffer from depression, especially since you can be so hard on yourself. You seldom take your feelings at face value, preferring a methodical approach to understanding your emotions instead of just letting yourself feel them. You also pressure yourself to "just get over it," which can lead you to fall into an emotional rut without even knowing it. Sometimes this disconnect between mind and body will manifest as sickness, with unresolved emotional distress actually causing physical symptoms, especially in your joints, bones and teeth.

To get off of the dark side and into the light, you have to learn to receive healthy support. Your Moon in Capricorn wants to have it all together, using every situation to get ahead, even in personal relationships. But without nurturing yourself and learning the fine art of asking for help, your power source is significantly depleted. You have to find times to let go of needing control and just be. You don't have to do it all yourself. Conversely, you don't have to expect anyone else to take care of you. Too much suffering for the sake of a relationship deprives the world of your power. Maintaining a loving relationship takes hard work, but it shouldn't take all the fun out of life.

Striking the balance between giving and receiving is the key to your happiness. Make time in your life for emotional check-ins with yourself and loved ones. Put it on your calendar. You may want to implement a regular practice that works for you. Do some journaling, practice insight meditation, or make a fancy wheel chart with color-coded sections for each emotion ("Today I feel _____"). Capricorn loves that kind of structure. Letting your emotions have equal time with your worldly goals will activate even more discipline and productivity.

The Goddess Within: Hera

The Moon in Capricorn has an affinity with the Great Goddess Hera, the Mother of the Gods. In Greek myth, Hera is known for her loyalty to the widely wandering Zeus and the revenge she takes on his various lovers. But her roots are deeper than the Greek pantheon. In her more ancient forms, she is revered as a goddess who rules over time and the stages of womanhood. Throughout her many stories, we can find a common thread in her commitment to building healthy systems, whether that's seen as society and the sanctity of marriage, or in the natural world where each part works responsibly to foster the wellbeing of the whole. Through her, the entire cycle of the feminine is honored: wildness, fertility and death; the freedom of youth and the responsibility of the mother.

She speaks:

"I am the sovereign one who serves none, and I am the servant of All. I move mountains and attend to the smallest bird. I have endured assimilation and sought peace through isolation, but still I endure.

"My true face is compassion. Unchain me and my fierceness manifests in protection of the Natural Order. If you commit to knowing me, you can take apart the structures of confinement that teach you that order is controlled and regulated. Discover another

order that moves and changes, yet remains stable through the ages. Freedom comes when you provide healthy boundaries for your work. Stability comes when you allow for and respond to change"

EXPLORATION

As a favorite of Hera, you have a special key that unlocks the door of responsible authority. To work with her and tap into the well of her power, go to wild places and look for the patterns there, the way each being has its place. Go to an urban landscape and contemplate the infrastructure that steadies the manmade environment.

To find out more about the power of the goddess within you, consider the following suggestions and questions:

How are the environments you visit different and how are they the same?

What are you committed to?

What do you see in the world that you want to flourish?

How can you support yourself without depriving others of happiness and liberty?

What would you be doing if you knew you could not fail?

Moon in Aquarius

♒

- Your Natural Resource: Vision
- Your Art of Loving: Cooperation
- The Dark Side of the Moon: Detachment
- The Goddess Within: Ix Chel

Aquarius is the sign of the visionary, the idealist and the humanitarian. With your Moon in this airy sign, your reservoir of power is a natural vision that draws you to projects and people that make a difference in the world. You have inner resources of curiosity and compassion, as well as an electric energy that sparks an urge to discover new territory. At your core, you are wild and free, liberated from the confines of authoritarian structures and hierarchies of power. And you want others to be free as well. You love to talk theory with friends and may have a hard time with committing to a single action. But when you are taking care of your needs and being honest with yourself about your true feelings, you can indeed change the world. However you spark that change, it depends upon giving yourself space to feel and taking risks to make friends, collaborate and cooperate. This Moon needs excitement and change but not for the sake of change like other signs; this desire comes from a vision to perpetuate the highest quality of life for all people.

You will feel more comfortable and secure if you intellectually process your emotions rather than getting swept away by them. The danger here is that you never allow yourself to actually feel those emotions, so you end up disconnected from your body. This can lead to trouble physically, as unacknowledged anxiety or depression ends up manifesting chronic illness. It can also make you shy of diving into deeper intimacy with others because you fear the lack of control when big emotions come to the surface.

You may feel you have an inner roadmap to utopia and therefore don't spend a lot of time on the superficial details of day-to-day living. You live in the big picture. Your home will reflect this in its simplicity, but will also show your eccentric side with unusual art or odd conversation pieces. Being a visionary means focusing on the future, so you often want the latest technology to keep you up on news and trends. But this attention to the future could just as easily lead you to a lifestyle of voluntary simplicity in order to do your part to preserve resources for future generations. You definitely want to be a part of a community that shares your high ideals, and so communal living or other cooperative structures that help people share their resources may appeal to you. Whatever the case, you need a living space that can bring people together to talk, dream and work together. Your garden can be just as wild as you are, with overgrown native flora welcoming wildlife and creating a space where natural order prevails.

Relationships and the Art of Loving: Cooperation

With the Moon in Aquarius, your mother or other primary caregiver may have been an energizing and innovative force, but it's also possible that she never seemed fully present. Early experiences gave you the sense that the world was an exciting but unpredictable place. Support given may have been more intellectual and dispassionate at times.

This Mother Moon may have seemed more like a friend to you than a mother, providing invaluable guidance in your most trying times. But an erratic upbringing may have created a subconscious desire for normalcy and an overwhelming desire to feel accepted. Your family life seemed "different" somehow, and you yourself may have struggled with feeling out of place within your own family or community. A natural shyness coupled with curiosity in human behavior may have sent you retreating into your own mind for solace and stability.

This emotional inheritance includes the gift of seeing unconventional approaches to the challenges of human relationships. You want to understand where people are coming from, so you learn all you can about the social, economic and political conditions that shape human behavior. You have high ideals about human relationships, so it's easy for people to disappoint you, and for you to disappoint yourself. But when you can move past the purely intellectual theories and into the living world of emotional expression, you can begin to see yourself and others with more forgiveness and acceptance. This is where real cooperation begins.

You crave freedom and the unexpected, which might translate into "not ready to commit." But you are here to discover innovative new approaches to healthy human relationships. To own your power in relationships, you have to develop a sense that commitment isn't static. You need your relationships to evolve with you. It's up to you to keep your finger on the pulse of your own dreams and to initiate frank discussions if you feel those dreams are hampered in any way by assumed relationship roles. With your unusual sense of humor and willingness not to take yourself too seriously, you can often find loving approaches to envision the next phase of life with your partner or community.

You have a natural ability to bring out the best in others, as long as you yourself are not blocking your emotional side by over-intellectualizing things. The Moon in Aquarius has a role to play in bringing about more equitable and compassionate human relationships, and you start to feed this larger goal when you allow yourself to listen to your body and act on that information.

The key to your art of loving is cooperation. This includes the inner cooperation of letting your heart and mind work together to keep you healthy. Push yourself to consciously feel and express your emotions as they surface. It's okay if you need to take space sometimes to process, as long as you don't use this as a cover for not really dealing with painful experiences and feelings. Don't leave your loved ones waiting for resolution.

A blocked Aquarius Moon can pretend everything is all right, living in the world of ideas and vision. But a bit of commitment to tackling uncomfortable problems will lead to greater satisfaction in relationships, as well as unlocking your natural vision to come up with new solutions to old power struggles. When you see others as potential allies, it awakens this visionary cooperative spirit and helps you build relationships that elevate humanity.

The Dark Side of the Moon: Detachment

You are brimming with ideas and sometimes this can manifest as a need to be constantly "doing something." Whenever you do stop to think, you inevitably come up with a whole new list of errands, projects and ideas. Physically, this translates into nervous legs and an inability to relax. If you suffer from anxiety and insomnia, it could be another signal that your Moon is blocked.

Your high regard for objectivity sometimes comes off as just plain cold. When you feel yourself "rising above" a situation, check in to see if you are feeling fear. The Moon in Aquarius can sometimes err on the side of detachment out of anxiety that emotions will lead to erratic, overwhelming situations. While emotions often defy rational explanations, you have a desire to process things intellectually in order to feel secure. But when your loved ones are expressing what they feel, it's not the time to theorize. Too much objectivity can be invalidating when sensitivity and compassion are called for.

You want to shake people out of their habits, so you sometimes do things purely for the sake of shock and rebellion. This is part of your gift to the world, because we all benefit from being awakened from numbing routine every now and then. But sometimes the confrontation you create distances people who could be your allies. You probably can't help but succumb to that urge to rebel, just don't get all defensive and frustrated when others find your behavior off-putting. You may even rebel against your own beliefs and sabotage worthwhile commitments you've made to others. Be careful of sowing only destruction without regard for what's already been created or what could be.

When your ideals of cooperation become dogmatic beliefs, you end up doing the opposite of your best intentions and actually ostracize others. You may want to be open and flexible to new ways, but truth be told, you often think that your way is the best way. When you get super attached to your beliefs, you block the natural visionary awakener within you. You may know the best way to get there, but it will take everyone's commitment and excitement to pull it off.

To step out of the darkness and into the light, you have to remember that the process is just as important as the product, and that the practice of cooperation is actually the best way for your natural vision to get translated into action.

The Goddess Within: Ix Chel

As the Lunar Goddess of the Maya people, Ix Chel would not be tamed by social convention or threat of parental retribution. She would have it her way, regardless of the consequences. In her stories we find both romantic entanglements and noble quests to help ease the suffering of humans. Her name means "Lady Rainbow," and she is just as colorful as the name implies. She has many aspects, one of which pours out the waters of life, destroying the old order and making way for the next age. Ix Chel rules over creativity, health, magic, water and weaving.

She speaks:

"You are a thread in my blanket sky. You are a thread and the weaver, too, learning to know your own mind and your own longing so that you may be free, so that you may join with other threads weaving together a new world.

"Remember that you are in a body and take care of that body. When the electricity of ideas threatens to pull you apart, rest in the gravity of the planet and know you are held.

"Remember that you are one thread and that there are many others weaving too. You can't do it alone. You only have to do your part in the grand design. Be like a rainbow, the bridge that connects Water and Air, the bridge between feeling and idea, between love and action."

EXPLORATION

Ix Chel connects you to the web of life and the web of ideas. She can help you vibrate with the potency of your visions while gently reminding you to take care of your nervous system. She is a bridge, and as such must be able to withstand enormous pressures without crumbling to the chasm below. Let her show you the way to balance between the present and future without fracturing into a million pieces.

To find out more about the power of the goddess within you, explore these questions:

What emotions frighten you?

In what ways do you block freedom, and in what ways do you foster it?

What's your highest vision for yourself, your community, the planet?

Are there ways in which your mind controls rather than supports your vision?

What do you need to stay grounded, healthy and calm? Do you make space in your life for this?

Moon in Pisces

- Your Natural Resource: Compassion
- Your Art of Loving: Higher love
- The Dark Side of the Moon: The harsh light of day
- The Goddess Within: Green Tara

The Moon finds a soft place to land in the waters of Pisces. Pisces asks how we can tap into universal love and surrender to the natural flow of life. With your Moon in Pisces, you have a natural sensitivity and possibly psychic abilities that tap you into an inner reservoir of compassion. Your strong inclination toward the mystical enables you to see beauty everywhere. When you focus on cultivating this innate reverence for the spiritual side, you can feel confident that a greater power directs your life. When your Moon is blocked, you feel isolated from others and struggle to see the point of anything. If this is the case, then your world becomes a lesson in suffering that threatens to pull you into a web of inaction and apathy. For you, the path of wellness must include time to reflect, to meditate and to use your imagination to create poetry, music or dance. The creative process is itself incredibly healing, and it is one of the many ways you replenish your natural resources and inspire others. Though you may have a decidedly introverted personality, it's important for you to take the risk of reaching out to others. Your tendency to withdraw from the world helps connect you to the vast, loving power of the Divine, but it can also disconnect you from the loving support of other humans striving to create healthy, compassionate relationships.

The Moon indicates how you react instinctively to situations, and Pisces reacts with gentleness. You are seeking the truth beyond illusion so that you can feel you really belong. Your security comes from trusting your Higher Truth regardless of how others see the world. Your power flows freely when you take that higher vision and put it into action by serving others, possibly through healing, the arts or spiritual activism. Your intuition and dreams are important sources of information. Because you are more innately attuned to the realms of the subconscious and collective unconscious, you can be moody and unpredictable. Feelings arise very quickly from your watery depths and can just as easily subside again into the void. Your task is to let them flow without getting caught in the confusing contradictions they impart. You must also be aware of taking on other people's feelings or picking up subtle energies from the environment.

Creating a safe haven can go a long way in helping you restore yourself when you've absorbed way too much suffering from the world. Under your soft, artistic direction, your home becomes an enchanted hideaway. Because you feel so much and so deeply, you need a place to reconnect to your own Higher Truth. Taking long, healing baths with lavender, rosemary or other purifying herbs cleanses your body as well as your soul. Make your bathroom into a mini-retreat center, with glowing candles and transcendent music. To satisfy your need to escape from the harsh light of day, you may want a movie room to draw you into fantastic stories or a meditation room to act as a cord to the Limitless Divine. Your garden can be another way you honor your mystical side, by creating a living altar with sacred plants, rocks and flowing water. Let your creativity and imagination guide you in transforming your living space into a sacred temple. When you surround yourself with fantastic images, healing colors and sacred objects, you will feel healthier and awaken your natural compassion.

Relationships and the Art of Loving: Higher Love

The lines of Mother and Child are blurry with a Pisces Moon. You may have perceived your mother or other primary caregiver through rose-colored glasses. This Mother Moon often welcomes a child's world of pretend and fantasy. You may have been encouraged to write, daydream, play music, or dance. As a child you may have learned the importance of serving and responding to others when there was need, but this ability relied on a lack of boundaries. Your caregivers might have had a sensitivity that made them unavailable at times, going off into their own worlds and leaving you with a stark absence of motherly support. With your Moon in Pisces, you could have had the very real responsibility of caring for your mother through ill health. Early childhood experiences passed on to you the idea that relationships contain the possibility of transcendence. You may still be seeking this seed of salvation through relationships, either by sacrificing your own dreams for the sake of another or identifying with an ideal that can never be realized.

To own your power in relationships, you have to bravely confront the illusions you have about love. Relationships are full of difficult compromise, partners have warty insides and bad breath, and there's not always a happily-ever-after. Your gifts of sensitivity and compassion make you a good listener, a romantic lover, and an incredibly loving, supportive partner. But when you mistake the ideal for the real, you may end up using those skills to manipulate others. You have such a love of romance that you may not even notice how terrible a relationship actually is.

The key to your art of loving is using your natural sensitivity to recognize what's really going on. When you are honest about your own emotional needs, you can remove the confusion that arises from taking on someone else's subconscious desires and unexpressed emotions. You can't expect any one person to fulfill all of your dreams, nor should you allow others to take advantage of your compassionate desire to serve.

The Dark Side of the Moon: The Harsh Light of Day

Both the Moon and Neptune, the planet that rules Pisces, uphold the notion that collective needs trump individual desires. Together, they can beautifully envision the possibility of mutually beneficial networks of support. But they can also create a lopsided dynamic that leads to one of your biggest challenges: the victim-savior complex. Your emotional security depends upon feeling spiritually connected, and when this need attaches to another person, you can become entangled in unhealthy relationships. Letting yourself be victimized out of a desire to transcend suffering; thinking you can "save" someone if you love them the right way; completely ignoring another's needs in favor of only seeing your romantic ideal – these are some of the ways this complex dynamic can manifest. To step into the light, you have to be willing to surrender, and that takes hard work. Check in to see if you have any attachments to suffering out of a belief that it is noble. Examine whether you have friends and partners who share your commitment to emotional expression. Get honest about the expectations you have of romantic relationships, friendships and family members. When you have done this, you will see the behaviors you need to let go of and can begin taking steps to get your power back.

With your Moon in Pisces, you are prone to coping with the pain of living by numbing out, which manifests as eating sweets, drinking alcohol or taking other mood and consciousness-altering substances. You may also be an expert at leaving your body – a kind of mild disassociation or astral projection – in order to escape from personal and transpersonal pain. You are a nostalgic creature, and even when events in the past were traumatic or intense, you may cling to them out of the sense that they contain some essential truth or noble purpose. In order to let your Moon flow through you rather than carry you away, you have to heal from the past, forgiving yourself and others for the parts they played in your suffering. Spend time replenishing your soul in healthy ways, cleansing your waters so to speak. Meditation, listening to or playing music with friends, writing about your past, spiritual counseling – any of these mediums can tap you into the Universal Source without removing all your necessary human boundaries.

People with a Pisces Moon channel the energy of healing into all sorts of careers, so it is especially important to learn how to regularly clear off negative energy and check in with what you're carrying. You feel other people's pain in your own body. Because of your natural compassion and sympathy, you can attract some pretty needy and troubled people. You can't help everyone, and you can't help anyone if you're denying your own human limitations. When you hear the cries of world but feel powerless to help, you may try "breathing through" by imagining the pain as a ribbon of breath moving into you and then breathing it out through your heart. Simple spiritual practices like this go a long way in helping you see that you have a role to play in the healing of our world, but you cannot carry it all.

You have a body. It carries within it great pain and great revelation. It is the vehicle through which you are able to manifest your highest ideals of beauty and love. Make sure you take care of it.

The Goddess Within: Green Tara

Green Tara, the Buddhist Goddess of active compassion, began her existence as a human, and became a goddess when she achieved enlightenment but refused to enter Nirvana until all souls were liberated. This is the vow of the Bodhisattva. Tara represents the unquenchable hunger that propels all life. She is a star that guides people to their destinations. She is always available to help us come home to ourselves, and to understand that behind all appearances exists the dance of creation that we can enter playfully when we are willing to master our own illusions and limitations. Green Tara is fierce as well as compassionate, and she may shake you with fear if your heart isn't open to her. If you can stay simultaneously present and active, you will see behind her terrifying eyes into the true heart of love.

She speaks:

"I will teach you my mantra, which has no beginning or end: sweetness, softness, terror, dinner, roses, wildfires, earthquakes, harvests, calm waters, safe passages, violence, compassion, inequality, greed, cloud bursts, vacant lots, homelessness, giving, laughter, lies, politics, transformation, religion, change, habit, indecision, popularity, privilege, cancer, newborn, poverty, first kiss, ancient trees, sexual pleasure, slavery, weakness, sacraments, television, hotdogs, wind chimes, open doors, open hands, open hearts.

"Open like me to everything possible, everything being born, everything dying. Let everything happen to you. Do not deny life. Do not hide from your own heart or from those who confound you. And when you feel your heart ready to burst or break, then let it call you to action. Trust yourself. You will know the right thing to do. Trust in your Higher Truth like you trust the Earth to move around the Sun."

EXPLORATION

When Green Tara dances into your life, it is time to rejoice in your own spirit and be free of limitations. Honoring your Moon means being fluid like water. You have great empathy and insight into the human condition, but that doesn't mean you have to let every feeling take you over. When you feel too full, find a way to become empty again. Take care of yourself just as much as you take care of others, and vice versa.

To find out more about the power of the goddess within you, explore these questions:

How do I blur the lines between fantasy and reality?

When my heart is breaking, whom do I count on for support?

What are the ways I long to heal and nurture others?

In my relationships, do I tend to fall into the role of victim or the role of savior?

What events in my life have made me doubt my abilities to take care of myself and others, and how can I heal from those moments?

Moon by House

The **houses** are an important part of looking at the whole of a Natal Chart. In general, the houses show us *where* the action is. Each house governs an area of life. Depending on the house in which it is placed, each planet will have a specific sphere of activity through which it will find its most natural expression or face its fiercest battles.

You don't have to be an astrologer to make use of the insights given by the houses. Again, you can easily find out which House contains your Moon by getting your chart cast for free from a website like *www.astro.com* or visiting your local astrologer. [See Appendix A in back of book for details.]

Each house in your natal chart is its own theater, with the planets contained in them like the actors in a play. They show us the different areas of life in which we "act out" the energies of the signs and planets – such as home, school, career or religion. The house that contains your Moon tells you about the places and people that will have the greatest influence on your emotional wellbeing.

In order to fully utilize the natural resource described by your Moon Sign, you must seek out those realms described by your Moon's House and be prepared to meet in them the watery, mysterious Moon.

Moon in First House/Moon on the Ascendant
Feeling your Way

With your Moon in the First House of Identity, you strongly embody the qualities of the Moon itself. You are naturally sensitive and receptive to other people and situations. It is especially important that you allow your emotions and feeling states to be expressed, as withholding expression can lead you to question your own self-worth and affect you physically. You may often be looking for clues about who you are based on these emotional states. You will also look to relationships with a sharper eye for information about your sense of self.

For you, the Moon's need to belong can distort your sense of individuality. This can swing from over-asserting your ideas and feelings to confusion about who you are except in relation to others. The First House rules appearance, and with the Moon here you may change your style and clothes to fit the situation. People may not recognize you in a new environment, as you can be a sort of chameleon. This does not necessarily mean that you don't stand out, but you will want to express your individuality in a way that suits the occasion and leads you to a sense of belonging.

This placement imparts great skill at sensing what's going on with others and the environment. It creates a strong link between emotional instinct and action. You can tune in to what loved ones need and then create subtle shifts in the energy to make a more positive emotional space. You may use this skill gladly for others' benefit, but it is often utilized to fulfill your own desire to feel safe. You may exert an aura of authority whose source seems to come from some collective body of wisdom. Be careful of using this intuitive power to exert too much control over your life and other people's affairs. Your own need to belong and/or to be right can severely cloud your objectivity.

The Moon in the First House can impart a strong trust in your own instincts. Even though you may mold yourself to ideas of what others want you to be, the goal is to get your needs met. You can be sure that your intuition is right on when you feed and honor the Moon with what nurtures you as described in your Moon Sign section. To you, life is ultimately about relating to others in a way that makes you feel safe and loved, and respecting the cycles that move through you. You have a special opportunity to restore the Moon – our instinctual, emotional nature – to a position of respect and reverence because you can easily channel its lunar light through you.

Moon in Second House
Emotional Resources

With your Moon in the Second House of Resources and Possessions, you may rely on financial wealth, property, or other material structures to make you feel secure and emotionally available. But what you may really be seeking is a sense of safety that can only come from within – a place beyond material comfort and rooted in love. With the moon in play, you may place a high value on your emotions, family, and home. Your confidence may be strongly linked to loved ones, or to actual physical possessions that instill in you the memories and feelings of good times. This is a lesson in surrender in some ways, as you learn to find the intrinsic value hidden within the object.

The material world is changeable; just as the Moon rides from sliver to circle in our sky, so do our lives wax and wane through times thick and thin. For you, it may be difficult to let go of your inherited family or cultural values, but you may have to in order to find a comfortable security that fits your current lifestyle. This is a placement that denotes fluctuation of resources, but it also imparts with it the adaptability and resourcefulness to meet the changing conditions of your life. If you are willing to learn the fine art of surrendering what you think you need, you will find what truly supports you.

You may have exceptional instincts for the cycles of finance, real estate and markets, and you can use these skills in your work. You can find comfort in collecting antiques or in tending the history and lineage of your family. Your home will most likely be filled with precious keepsakes or important mementos. For you, something has value because of the feeling behind it and the history that it holds.

Overall, this placement speaks of the opportunity to rediscover the ancient wisdom of impermanence. When you tap into your inner resources and acknowledge the core wealth of skills that you possess, you can find a stability that transcends "the slings and arrows of outrageous fortune." Your Moon in the Second House may subconsciously seek physical representations of security, but it is when you embrace change that you discover your real inner wealth: recognition of the value of love behind actions and objects.

Moon in Third House
Emotional Intelligence

With the Moon in the Third House, you are here to discover how to use your intellect to understand your heart. You may spend much of your life involved with places of learning that stimulate your curiosity, as you are a natural student. Finding out how things work and accumulating information will give you a sense of security as you walk through the world.

The Third House rules the mind, communication and your environment. You may communicate more freely about your emotions than others, and having this closeness with others is essential to unlocking your truth and gifts. Friends, siblings and even neighbors are an important source of guidance in matters of the heart. You are friendly and can quickly put people at ease with your genuine rapport. With the Moon here, you may have a natural curiosity about what makes people tick. You need to know how others are feeling in order to feel secure in yourself, but be careful of assuming too much.

You are naturally sensitive to the power of thoughts and will see the world through the eyes of whatever mood has taken you. More so than other people, you create your own reality, because what you feel strongly colors how you perceive your immediate environment. When you are feeling grounded and happy, this gift can manifest an infinite supply of interesting people and places for you to explore. But if you are feeling painful, negative emotions, you could unconsciously hurt those you care about or create challenging situations. When you feed your Moon, you can more easily access your emotional intelligence and differentiate between your own moods and your environment. Texting or talking with good friends, surfing the Internet, or taking a class are some of the ways that you might recharge your batteries.

The Moon in the Third House gives you insight into the hidden thoughts and feelings of others, so use it carefully and with compassion. You were born to listen and to help others feel comfortable about their emotions, their bodies and their needs. Activities that support your Moon in the Third House are writing and journaling, taking classes, teaching and public speaking. See how you can blend these intellectual pursuits with your more sensitive side, like researching your ancestral lineage, writing about your dreams or taking a class in the intuitive arts.

Moon in Fourth House/Moon on the IC
Feeling at Home

The Moon is the natural ruler of the Fourth House of home, roots and family. For you, finding security means gravitating toward experiences that take you deep within yourself in order to discover the essential truths that shape you. Your family and culture of origin will have a powerful impact on your sense of identity and wellbeing. Regardless of the actual events of your upbringing, you may look back on your childhood with longing and fondness, for the past holds great sway over your current emotional behavior.

To honor your Moon – the seat of your soul – you may instinctively be drawn to create a loving, nurturing home that serves as a place to restore yourself. Whether through psychological exploration, meditation or dream work, understanding the subtle energies that shift your perceptions and guide your actions can help you feel more stable and naturally loving. You most likely display a keen sensitivity to your family's needs and will be able to offer nurturing and support to fit those needs, provided that there are no other astrological aspects that block such free expression. Changes in your home may lead to extreme anxiety, but you also have the skill of adaptability to adjust to those changes if you let yourself move through your feelings.

In less positive expressions of a Fourth House Moon, you might give too much of your power away to others in an effort to blend in. Childhood experiences and early perceptions of your Mother or other primary caregiver can continue to hold you to patterns of behavior in your adult relationships that block you from freely expressing your current emotional needs. Family and home are vital sources of reflection for you, but learning how to acknowledge these important emotional connections without pinning your whole identity onto them will serve your deeper quest to understand who you are.

Overall, this placement is about taking root, and you need to cultivate enough awareness to find healthy soil. Your lunar journey leads you to home. As poet Robert Frost wrote in *The Death of the Hired Man*, "Home is the place where, when you have to go there, they have to take you in." Finding refuge for you means summoning total acceptance for the forces that have shaped you without holding onto any negative patterns that they may have created. To flow is your gift, and you can use it to create vibrant home and family structures full of love.

Moon in Fifth House
Feeling Special

With your Moon in the Fifth House of self-expression and romance, you may display natural artistic talent, and this impulse to create is what leads you toward emotional security. Whatever works of art you generate – paintings, meals or even children – they will come from your soul and heartfelt emotions. For you, feeling loved and secure can mean receiving plenty of attention or special recognition for your accomplishments. You will subconsciously seek activities that you can pour your whole self into and specifically those ruled by the Fifth House, such as creative hobbies, physically challenging sports, child-rearing or romantic involvement.

Growing up, you may have felt driven to express your uniqueness in order to feel worthy of love from caregivers. In your adult relationships, the dynamics of your own upbringing can rear up as you seek to untangle any unresolved issues with your mother or other primary caregivers. Creating emotionally dramatic displays is one way you may have learned to be the center of attention. These issues can be pushed to the forefront in relationships with your children or children in general. Children, who are natural artists, can be your teachers and an important source of reflection and inspiration for you.

Honoring your Fifth House Moon means letting yourself tap into a sense of play. You are learning how to give confident expression of your emotional needs and artistic instincts. Finding an outlet that speaks to you is vital to your sense of security. Again, this can take many forms, and the important thing is that it awakens your natural passion and excitement for living. Providing healthy outlets for this inner radiance can reveal a hidden resource of leadership, which will flow from you with generosity and warmth.

Overall, this placement can connect you into a sense that you are a child of the Universe, worthy of love and endowed with your own special talents. Whether in the home or out in the world, your Moon will draw you toward authentic emotional expression that comes straight from the heart. Connect to your heart's desire in order to find creatively rewarding avenues for self-expression. Doing so will provide you with a supportive foundation so that you can shine more of your light and love on others.

Moon in Sixth House
Body of Feeling

With your Moon in the Sixth House, you will find greater inner peace when you engage in daily rituals that connect emotional, physical and intellectual wellness. The Sixth House rules such diverse domains as the body, nutrition, servants, small pets and service work. If we look closer, we can see that these areas are united by a thread of how we maintain and organize ourselves and our world. For you, special attention should be given to your body and the physical manifestations of your emotions. It's possible that you have to deal with health problems in your genetic line, but the Moon here could also indicate that you are learning how your family's emotional inheritance relates to physical illness. Dietary restrictions, eating disorders and allergies are sometimes common indications that you need more regular practices to help you deal with daily stresses.

The Moon shows us where we are naturally responsive, and with yours in the Sixth House, your body can be a treasure trove of insight. You easily pick up emotional information from the people and places around you. It's important for you to check in with your body in order to develop accurate responses to current situations. Having a daily routine can facilitate such clear communication between your body and mind. Healthy eating choices, a meditation practice or simply stretching your body can help you feel grounded and emotionally stable.

You may be especially sensitive to work-related events and co-workers. Changes with your job can upset your whole sense of order. You can also find refuge through serving others and may throw yourself into your job when other areas of your life are stressing you out. Having a pet or other connection with animals can calm your soul and help you cope, as well as supply you with something tangible to take care of.

Overall, this placement indicates that you have a special opportunity to help restore balance between the emotional, physical and intellectual realms. Your soul craves a healthy relationship between body and mind. The more you provide yourself with daily practices that maintain these connections, the more you can offer healing to the larger world.

Moon in Seventh House/Moon Conjunct DC
Feeling the Other

With your Moon in the Seventh House of Relationships, you may subconsciously seek inner security in the arms of another. You may be drawn to partners and friends through a healthy desire to expand your sense of self. But you could also be driven by emotional complexes and internal conflicts that only come to awareness through projection or when reflected back to you by loved ones. It's probably a little of both, but the tendency of the Moon here is to be a bit over-adaptive to the needs of others in order to feel inner peace.

For you, committed relationships may be the place you look for the Moon. If you have any resistance to owning your own Moon and tending to your emotions, instincts and home, then you may look for someone else who's in touch with their feeling nature. There's nothing wrong with searching for a partner who is caring, receptive and nurturing, but you have to take responsibility for your own feeling as well. Here, we are deeply in the domain of Moon as Mother. You may project issues surrounding the care you received as a child onto your adult relationships as you seek to resolve them.

The house that holds the Moon shows us where we are particularly sensitive to the people and places in our lives. In the Seventh House, you have the opportunity to tune into the emotional wavelength of spouses, close friends or business partners. This can make you incredibly responsive and adaptable in these relationships. But you must be careful of over-accommodating or repressing your emotions for the sake of stability. This can lead to built-up resentment. Because of the changing nature of the Moon in an Airy House, you may be attracted to partners who are restless, emotionally detached or unstable, or you yourself may embody these qualities. You are learning how to face up to your feeling nature and to see others accurately at the same time. Blending these two streams makes the current of your life even stronger.

Overall, this placement gives you the opportunity to find heartfelt and deep emotional connections in your committed relationships. To consciously meet "the Other" is to meet your own shadow and unexpressed parts. Through relationships and healthy engagement when conflict arises, you will discover a true sense of self and belonging.

Moon in Eighth House
Emotional Intimacy

With your Moon in the Eighth House, you embody a complex and watery domain that tunes you into the undercurrents of life. The Eighth House is often referred to as the House of Sex, Death and Other People's Money (such as inheritances); the thread that links all three is the unseen web of interconnections. You most likely have an intuitive and deep understanding of the intimacy required to share such exchanges of energy. This can make you eerily insightful in everything from personal relationships to financial and social trends.

You may feel compelled to investigate what's hidden. This includes your own psychology, family skeletons or even cultural taboos, in order to bring them to an eventual resolution. This Moon seeks security through intimate or sexual partners, through shared resources, and even through walking on the dark side of life. You are often resourceful and perceptive in situations of crises and intense transformation. You may be attracted to situations that are exhilarating or even dangerous in order to feel emotionally alive. At any rate, you can lead yourself and others to healing when you work consciously with hidden, unexpressed emotions.

Part of this Moon's lesson is about finding the internal resources to heal and transcend trauma. You can often find real emotional security when you learn to surrender some of your need for control. Delving into the Eighth House toolbox, you will find psychic gifts and other divination tools; esoteric spiritual practices that broaden your sense of self; a wide range of healthy sexual expression; and explorations of birth, death and other rites of passage. For you, your sense of personal safety can spring from the freedom to experience all sides of life, from continually shedding your skin to be born into someone new.

Overall, this placement asks of you to find the willingness to soften some of your boundaries without losing yourself completely. When you let go of intentionally manipulative or fear-based behavior, you can begin to claim the true power of deep intimacy. Let yourself explore the unseen world that pulses all around us. You have a special opportunity to reveal exactly what needs to be healed emotionally and psychically and send those ripples of awakening consciousness out into the world.

Moon in Ninth House
Feeling Expansive

With your Moon in the Ninth House of Philosophy, Religion and Law, your sense of emotional security comes from being able to see the bigger picture and continually broaden your perspectives. You may be instinctively drawn to institutions of higher education, traveling or spiritual practice in order to fulfill those intrinsic needs. Having faith in something can help you carve out a solid foundation for your life, whether that faith is in a just and compassionate humanity or a just and compassionate god. Your family or culture's religious beliefs – or lack thereof – will play an important role in shaping your explorations.

For you, the Moon's need to belong can make you susceptible to the influences of teachers, gurus or others who seem to grasp vast and complex concepts. You yourself most likely possess an incredible intuitive understanding of symbols, philosophies and cultures, and this enables you to feel quite at home in a variety of situations. You are learning how to trust this wisdom without relying too much on external validation. But there is also the danger of clinging too tightly to your faith or belief systems out of the sense of order and security they provide for you. You can feed your moon healthy food whenever you engage in activities that expand your mind. Feeling safe and nurtured is a matter of principle for you, and you will be drawn to continue this quest for a spiritual home in order to meet your emotional needs.

Your relationships will find their strongest foundations when based on shared philosophical or spiritual beliefs. But you may also be attracted to those who can give you a very different perspective from your own. You may even choose to live in a foreign country for the same reason. Even if you stay close to home, your Moon will direct you to seek a diversity of human experiences.

Overall, this placement provides you with a special opportunity to expand the horizons of consciousness by awakening yourself and others to fundamental spiritual truths at the very core of all phenomena. In this way, home becomes a very big, very inclusive place with room for everyone at the table.

Moon in Tenth House/Moon Conjunct MC
Professional Moon

With your Moon in the Tenth House of Career and Social Role, you will most likely be sensitive to your reputation and how you are publicly perceived. In some ways, you are a professional Moon and may be drawn to work that utilizes the lunar qualities of nurturing and mothering, such as providing care, housing or healing to those who need it. Your emotional security and sense of safety is built from establishing prestige and recognition in your professional life. When you feel as though you are making a difference in the world, you are more confident and grounded in who you are.

For you, the Moon's need to belong could manifest as a heightened awareness of public opinion. Your career will bring your emotions to the surface and may be where you struggle with any unresolved issues from childhood. As a child, you were probably especially tuned in to how your mother or other primary caregiver dealt with her emotions and may have even felt a sense of responsibility for her wellbeing. In any case, you will subconsciously be drawn to work through issues about authority and accountability with your boss or the public.

A Tenth House Moon imparts the ability to feel out what society needs and then looks to fulfill those needs. Using your intuitive-emotional skills in your work will lead you to a deeper understanding of your own cycles of emotional needs. Your relationships as well may be colored by a desire for recognition and status. Partners may be valued for the service they provide to the larger world, and you may use your Moon to support and nurture their work instead of building your own empire. It's important for you to be aware of your own deep desires for public appreciation and to feed yourself in appropriate ways.

Overall, this Moon placement puts a powerful emphasis on building responsive structures that benefit society as a whole. You may feel pushed and pulled by the "madding crowd" as you seek to fulfill the endless needs of the world, and your emotions will both guide you and confound you as you feel challenged to work with something so personal in such a public way. But the ultimate gift of this placement is restoring the Moon to a place of honor and reverence, discovering the value of nurturing, compassion and the cyclical nature of time.

Moon in Eleventh House
Finding Community

With your Moon in the Eleventh House of Community, you may feel especially sensitive to the feelings and opinions of your friends, people in groups and humanity as a whole. This placement brings a heightened awareness of collective needs and goals, and you may seek out organizations concerned with nurturing common goals and supporting visions for the future. Belonging to a community that's bound by ideals and grand principles may be necessary for you to feel emotionally secure. When you are cooperating with others and listening to both feelings and ideas, you know you are on the right track.

This Moon placement can bring with it a slightly scattered attention, because you are a conduit for new ideas. Your natural sensitivity to the collective mind means you may have constantly shifting moods and feelings that correspond to current events or the opinions of others, even as your larger vision for the future remains intact. Because of your ability to blend in with different groups, you may excel at building coalitions and connections across a wide swath of society.

For you, friendships and group affiliations may be more important than settling down with one person. You may build your family from shared ideas, resources and projects rather than blood connections. The Eleventh House Moon is looking for relatedness, for the ways we can cooperate and recognize our inherent interconnections. This is an Air House, so the Moon here might generate a blur between feeling and thought. You may be more concerned with connecting through ideas rather than emotional displays. Your Moon can find its substance when you provide yourself with opportunities to work with others on social causes or other shared goals.

Overall, the Moon in the Eleventh House puts you in touch with our evolving human consciousness as you instinctively seek out the ways that your own wellbeing is more deeply fulfilled when linked with the wellbeing of others. However you choose to work with this energy, you can naturally and easily tune it to the global brain in order to learn from our shared human history and envision a vibrant, secure future.

Moon in Twelfth House
Ocean of Feeling

With your Moon in the Twelfth House of Dreams and the Collective Unconscious, you are endowed with an acute sensitivity to the feelings and moods of those around you, even people you are not personally connected to. You can pick up energy from the environment without knowing it, so it is vital for you to give yourself time to cleanse and recharge your soul. It may be useful for you to engage in regular energy work to clear away what doesn't belong to you or to visualize protective boundaries surrounding you as you go about your day-to-day work. You may have increased psychic abilities or illuminating dreams that serve as resources of information and self-knowledge.

For you, the Moon's need to belong can threaten to absorb you completely into an ego-less state. The degree to which you succumb to the waves of collective experiences depends largely on your Moon's Sign and other aspects. But regardless, you will most likely be vulnerable to the unexpressed feelings and desires of others, and may even have karmic or past life energy to tend for yourself or your family. You have to work to make your feelings conscious in order to master your personal emotional needs. Otherwise, these needs will emerge in deeply unconscious ways, and you may feel as if you have no control over your life.

From time to time, it will be important for you to withdraw from the world, such as by going on retreats or simply spending quiet weekends at home alone. This will help you differentiate between your feelings and the feelings of others. It will also help you to better serve others with your compassionate, healing skills if you understand the importance of caring for yourself. You may have been incredibly hooked into your Mother or other primary caregiver as a child, so it could be worth it to explore any lingering issues of dependency or secrecy associated with your childhood.

Overall, with a Twelfth House Moon, you have been given an opportunity to instinctively understand the deep undercurrents that run through the emotional world of the collective. You can use this sensitivity to bring healing and alleviate suffering on personal and even political levels. Finding constructive outlets for your intense feeling nature will enable you to walk between the worlds without getting caught in webs of illusion. Ecstatic spiritual practices, singing, writing, and working with your dreams are some of the ways you might consider working with your gifts and honoring the Moon in your life.

Aspects to the Moon

Aspects are the relationships that the planets in our Natal Chart have with one another. They can describe the ways various energies will work together. Sometimes, even energies with very different qualities will easily find balance and harmony, while other times we have to consciously strive toward discovering how two planets – two parts of ourselves – can get along with each other. In this section, the relationships of other planets to the Moon are discussed.

Aspects to your Moon tell you more about the conditioning you received in early childhood and what supports you or gets in the way of accessing loving, healthy power in your relationships. By working to make conscious the energies these aspects describe, you will feel the natural power of your Moon manifesting in positive ways rather than holding you hostage to early conditioning.

This chapter will look at "challenging aspects" or those that require some elbow grease, and "harmonious aspects" which are generally viewed as beneficial and easy. Wherever the Moon is in your Natal Chart, it will be making angles to other planets. For example, if I have the Moon at 15° Taurus, it will make a 90° aspect to any planets located at 15° Leo and/or Aquarius. (If you're unsure how to figure this out, you can consult the handy computer chart interpretations at *www.astro.com* or your friendly local astrologer.)

For simplicity, I will only address the Square (90°) & Opposition (180°) for challenging aspects and the Trine (120°) & Sextile (60°) for harmonious aspects. The Conjunction (0°) is a bit of a mixed bag. It can be both challenging and harmonious. If you have the Moon conjunct another planet in your chart, I suggest reading both sections to get a feel for what this placement means for you.

Keep in mind that it is often in the challenges that we find our greatest gifts. Challenging aspects are the places in our charts that energy pushes and pulls at us. And where there's that kind of friction, there's the opportunity to see the spark of the divine at work in our lives.

One way to work with the aspects is to think of the aspecting planet as being on your Moon's team. Some teammates, like Jupiter and Venus, may be more valuable and helpful than others. Some teammates have less energy or support to give than others. One page XX you will find a quick guide to reference the kind of energy each particular planet brings to the team. After you've read the section about your unique aspects to the Moon, it's a good idea to remind yourself about which Sign and House your Moon resides. When it comes down to, this is what your Moon requires and the other planets can either help or hinder the fulfillment of those needs.

Quick Guide to the Energy of the Planets:

The Planets – Planets are the *what* of the chart, a principle, ability or part of our mind/consciousness.

☉   **Sun**: Principle of creativity, ego, will, and self-image.

☿   **Mercury:** Principle of perception and communication.

♀   **Venus:** Principle of relationship, self-worth and values.

♂   **Mars:** Principle of desire, ability to assert one's self, conflict and separation.

♃   **Jupiter:** Principle of faith, growth, meaning and expansion.

♄   **Saturn:** Principle of work, structure, commitment and obstacles or blocks.

♅   **Uranus:** Principle of freedom, rebellion and individuality.

♆   **Neptune:** The collective unconscious, dreams, confusion and fantasy, spiritual aspirations.

♇   **Pluto:** Principle of deep transformation, the unknown, power and the underworld.

Moon to Sun Aspects
Trine, Sextile or Conjunction

Your inner nature is working in concert with your conscious self. The Sun represents our ego, our solar self, which strives to leave its mark on the world. The Moon's needs sometimes play second fiddle to the fiery passion of the Sun. But with the Moon and Sun in harmonious aspect, you are blessed with an easy pairing between what feeds you emotionally and what drives you to create. The challenge is to not fall into complacency by just assuming that all your needs will be met without any effort on your part.

Your early childhood experiences may have instilled in you an acceptance of yourself. A certain amount of unity and consistency gave you a foundation of self-confidence on which to build your budding personality. You have a natural ability to lead an outwardly rewarding life while maintaining emotional structures that support your internal needs.

Trust that when you give yourself what you need to feel secure and loved (the Moon), you will be better able to manifest your pure vision and desire (the Sun). Know that the opposite is also true, and the more you follow your passion, the more energy you will have to take care of your basic needs. With this aspect, you can tap into the feeling that you were conceived in love and trust, and therefore, all that follows is the fruit of that love. When you believe that, even through the difficult circumstances of life, you know the power to create is healing in and of itself. You are here to manifest the healing, creative energy that honors both the inner and outer worlds of humankind.

Moon to Sun Aspects
Square, Opposition and Conjunction

With your Moon in hard aspect to the Sun, you may struggle with trusting yourself. You look outside of yourself for answers, trying to define who you are by the people, places and experiences around you.

Conversely, you may rely too heavily on your own perceptions for guidance and grow confused by how others perceive you. The basic struggle here is between your needs and wants. The Moon gives you a sense of inner security, and when this is in conflict with your outer goals (the Sun), your life becomes a battle. When you honor your Moon and provide yourself with inner security as outlined in your "Sign and House" sections, you will be better able to tackle those bigger dreams that move you from passivity into action. If either the Moon or the Sun is given too much prominence, you will feel constantly out of balance and energetically depleted.

In your early childhood experiences, there may have been a sense of continuous conflict, and parents may have even separated. This reinforces your perception of adult relationships as an either/or choice between two opposing forces. Life may seem like a split of desires – the desire for security and the desire for self-expression – and caregivers probably visibly struggled with these insecurities.

With this aspect, you are here to discover the way to integrate the many diverse desires within you. You have to make room to respect the past and to learn from mistakes made then, without letting this unconsciously diminish your own possibilities for the future. Developing trust in yourself becomes a matter of survival, for you can easily fall into such a state of internal conflict that it becomes impossible to move ahead.

When you learn to juggle personal goals with more basic needs in your home life, you will do something that makes both you and your family proud.

Moon to Mercury Aspects
Trine, Sextile or Conjunction

With your Moon in a soft aspect with Mercury, you are supported by a natural common sense. You are a good listener, as you are innately sensitive and sympathetic to the needs of others. When you make an effort to utilize your gifts of communication, you will come to a deeper understanding of how to access the reservoir of power that your Moon Sign imparts.

In your early childhood, communicating emotional needs may have been encouraged, and this gave you a great head start in learning the openness and honesty required to sustain healthy relationships. In your adult relationships, you will need to be able to freely express yourself and to have a kind of daily check-in with loved ones about what's going on with you. This makes it easier for you to understand the ups and downs of your day-to-day life.

The Moon-Mercury together can sometimes create a voyeur, which means you have excellent skills of observation but also a tendency to be a bit emotionally detached from your own life and feelings. To access the gifts of this aspect, you have to consciously strive to communicate to others how you are feeling. When you do, you will find it easy to get to the heart of matters while maintaining friendly relationships. Focusing on the specific energies your Moon imparts to you will help you see which issues you need to communicate about and what sort of power struggles to watch out for in terms of the relationship between your feelings and your intellect.

Moon to Mercury Aspects
Square, Opposition and Conjunction

With your Moon in hard aspect to Mercury, you are working to balance your inner needs for emotional security with your need to make sense of the outside world. This aspect can lead to an unfocused mind that is so overly concerned with past events or other people's opinions that you find it almost impossible to move forward with any decision. You may be afraid that what you feel or think is somehow wrong and that expressing it will threaten your security. Sometimes this tendency can lead to denying emotions outright, lying or distorting the truth in order to soften the blow.

In your early childhood experiences, primary caregivers may not have been welcoming of forthright, honest communication about feelings. Maintaining a super-rational approach to emotional situations became the model for how to behave in relationships. You may still try to get a handle on your feelings before you communicate them to others, or you may feel so confused by them that you talk incessantly in an attempt to make others understand where you are coming from. What you really want is to see things more objectively.

With the Moon and Mercury stretching each other's limits, you are driven to achieve mental mastery over your feelings. This is challenging because you could feel totally foggy on what you actually think, so colored are your thoughts and feelings by your perceptions of the world around you and your own history. To balance these needs, you have to recognize that when your judgment is foggy, it may be time to refocus yourself with the kinds of activities your Moon Sign needs in order to feel balanced. Your practice is learning the subtle difference between the time to make a decision and the time to simply let your feelings flow.

Moon to Venus Aspects
Square, Opposition and Conjunction

With your Moon in soft aspect to Venus, you naturally honor the feminine principle in your life, whether this manifests as creativity, nurturing or social grace. Activities that seek to bring more beauty and balance to the world come fluidly through you. You are able to create win-win situations with your ability to cooperate and can also easily integrate your own needs for emotional security within your home, love life and career.

In your early childhood experiences, emotional outbursts may have been labeled as unpleasant and disorderly, and family members were encouraged to compromise. In your adult relationships, this may come up again as you work out how to express what you're really feeling and still maintain a sense of security. You may highly value your upbringing to the extent of being over-sentimental about family relationships. Learning how to respect your roots without turning a blind eye to the ways you were let down by caregivers will help you create realistic expectations of your current family life.

The challenge of this aspect manifests when you rely too heavily on charm or an ability to smooth out the rough edges, as this can make you subtly manipulative. Although everyone around you will think that you only have their best interests at heart, you could be subconsciously working things out to make sure your own needs are being met. This sets the stage for an easy material life, with resources flowing in when you need them. To support this aspect, make sure to surround yourself with the beauty you crave and discover how to express your inherent artistry through activities that feed your Moon Sign.

Moon to Venus Aspects
Square, Opposition and Conjunction

With your Moon in hard aspect to Venus, you are learning the importance of asserting your emotional needs. You may have difficulty in directly expressing your feelings. Your sensitive, adaptive nature means that you get hurt very easily and are also fearful of hurting the people you love. Your inner security falls apart when there's any hint of discord in your life. This aspect suggests a struggle to integrate your needs for emotional security with your longing for a beautiful, harmonious life. When things become too upsetting, you can retreat into charm and smiles, ignoring the real feelings you have bubbling up inside of you.

Your early childhood experiences may have been where you first learned this behavior, as emotional outbursts were most likely viewed as unpleasant and disorderly. You may have sought to maintain harmonious family relationships at all costs, and learned how to get what you wanted with grace and charm. In your adult relationships, you can use your sensitivity to help everyone feel heard and loved. When fear is driving you, you may subconsciously implement subtle manipulation to make sure that your own needs for security are met. This means repressing emotions, deflecting conflict or outright lying in order to preserve the peace.

With the hard aspect, your inner emotional needs may feel at constant odds with your view of relationships or your need to express yourself creatively. You may think that you have to withhold your emotions for the sake of relationship or that you can't balance your more artistic side with your basic needs for security.

To work with these energies, focus on giving yourself the kind of support your Moon Sign needs. When you value the resources imparted to you by your Moon, you can learn the fine art of integrating your emotional needs with what you want in a healthy relationship and fulfilling artistic life.

Moon to Mars Aspects
Trine, Sextile or Conjunction

With your Moon in a soft aspect to Mars, you have a natural ability to directly and honestly communicate about your feelings. You dislike emotional ambiguity and will look for friends and partners who aren't afraid to say what they feel. You don't block your instincts and are ready to take quick action in response to changes in the environment or within your own heart. The challenge presented by this aspect is not taking other people's feelings for granted. You are learning how to keep your instincts open while also understanding the importance of patience and sustained attention to ongoing issues in your home and love life.

Your early childhood environment may have been fast-paced, with caregivers given to quick emotional changes or even angry outbursts. You learned how to assert yourself and compete for affection in order to get the security you craved as a child. In your adult relationships, you are very sensitive to conflict. You probably don't shy away from it but will instead jump right in to get to the heart of matters. You easily express your sexual and emotional needs, but have to remember that the lines of communication go both ways. You go from impulse to action in the blink of an eye, and may need to slow down a bit in order to let your loved ones express their needs.

To activate the powerful potential of this aspect, you have to strive for consciousness around issues of emotional safety. When you give yourself room to honor your Moon, you can fully appreciate your sexuality and instinctive power to assert your desires.

Moon to Mars Aspects
Square, Opposition and Conjunction

With your Moon in hard aspect to Mars, asserting yourself may feel dangerous. Your Moon tells you what you need to feel safe and secure on the emotional front, while Mars isn't afraid of conflict and acts instinctively to get what it wants. When tension erupts between these two energies, you may feel as though you have no control in your life. You swing between withholding your anger or flying off the handle, trying to navigate a rough emotional terrain that threatens your basic needs for safety.

Your early childhood environment was rife with conflicts. Caregivers may have been explosive and volatile. Life may have been exciting, but it was also unstable, to the point that there may have been real physical threats to you or other family members. Issues around sexuality that formed in your childhood continue to frustrate you. You may have a subconscious expectation of conflict in your adult relationships as you work to reconcile your intense sexual and emotional desires with your need for safety.

To work with this aspect, you have to learn to accept the more volatile parts of yourself and see how anger can be a healthy part of your emotional life. If you repress your instincts, you will eventually blow up and create more damage than if you find measured ways to express yourself. Channeling energy into structured physical activity might help you feel emotionally safe enough to express your needs to others without fear of losing love or control. This aspect demands that you strive to understand the core of your emotional needs so they don't cause aggression, separation or unnecessary conflict.

Moon to Jupiter Aspects
Trine, Sextile or Conjunction

With Jupiter, the planet of expansion and belief, in harmonious aspect to your Moon, you have a powerful and joyful belief in yourself that can lead to truly sublime opportunities. The more you understand and appreciate your inner nature, the more you can expect to be shown the brighter side of life. You will naturally gravitate to situations that let you express your generous nature.

Your early childhood experiences urged you toward faith in order to feel secure. In their most positive expression, caregivers encouraged you to feel deeply and give your gifts to the world. Whether your child-self found faith in family or in a belief system, you will seek a similar spirit of free emotional expression and generosity in your adult relationships.

Whenever you feel blocked by external obstacles, you may simply choose to channel your energy somewhere else. Be careful of avoiding responsibility or indulging in a sense of entitlement. There's a danger of relying too heavily on your good looks and good luck to coast through life. If you do, you will deprive yourself and others of the depth of feeling you contain within you. When you make the effort to see the parts of yourself that are being deprived of full expression, you will find treasure even in the dark.

Moon to Jupiter Aspects
Square, Opposition and Conjunction

With the Moon in hard aspect to Jupiter, you exert great effort to ground your changing emotional needs into a system of belief that sustains you. You are trying to find a belief system that fosters security and also expands your knowledge of the world. You are learning how to balance the expansive, opportunity-making, faith-building Jupiter with the embodied, security-seeking, home-building Moon. Your ability to create opportunities may feel blocked whenever you have strong, unexpressed emotional needs.

Your early childhood experiences may have been colored by a sense of over-protection. Jupiter expands whatever it touches, so issues of security could have been pushed to the forefront in childhood. Caregivers may have tried to stay positive, at the expense of seeing what was really going on. In your adult relationships, you may err by trying too hard. You want to give people the best nurturing and love. This leads to making promises that are too big to keep or being over-protective and over-responsive to loved ones' needs.

The way to work with this aspect is to admit that you don't have all the answers. Realizing that sometimes life hands you a bad hand will help you deal with things more realistically. Remind yourself of what your Moon needs whenever you start to feel like you're at the bottom of the wheel. Feeding your Moon while stretching your horizons can help you learn that the wheel is always turning and that soon you will be on top again.

Moon to Saturn Aspects
Trine, Sextile or Conjunction

With the Moon in soft aspect to Saturn, you have a natural confidence in your ability to care for others as well as to help yourself to the kind of care you need. When you are in your rhythm, you will be able to provide both emotional and material support to loved ones with ease, thus feeding your own desire to have strong family bonds.

With this aspect, you learned the importance of sharing the workload early on. You may have had family traditions and clear definitions of family roles. This early exposure to the value of dependability in relationships makes you crave deep nurturance and family bonds in your adult relationships.

To work with this easy pairing of the Moon and Saturn, you have to be aware of emotional defenses that get in the way of what you are feeling. Safety may come in the form of family and a stable home, but looking within for love may help you find emotional security that's truly dependable. Feeding yourself with activities and energies outlined in your Moon by Sign and House sections will help you foster the inner reserves you need to create relationships built on mutual respect and support.

Moon to Saturn Aspects
Square, Opposition and Conjunction

With your Moon in hard aspect to Saturn, you are learning to define what makes you feel safe, and how this fosters emotional self-expression. The hard aspect to Saturn brings with it fear and insecurity, and in relationship to the Moon, you may fear being needy or not being able to provide for others. You may even feel that you don't deserve to be loved or that love is based on a sense of worth defined by your success or contributions to the whole.

In your early childhood experiences, you may have had to grow up quickly and share the workload with siblings and parents. You probably gained a strong sense of responsibility but may still crave a love that comes without criticism. In your adult relationships, you are working on letting go of defensive behaviors that may have their roots in childhood, such as emotional wall-building and harsh judgments of others.

To find the balance between Saturn and Moon, you have to learn how to look within for the unconditional love you crave, while still staying open enough to express emotional needs in relationships. This actually creates a loop that feeds itself, for when you express yourself, you can discover more clues to what you need to feel safe. Feeling safe is the key to building confidence and self-acceptance of emotional states. This aspect can put you through a ropes course in understanding how to foster relationships built on mutual respect and support while maintaining the integrity within yourself.

Moon to Uranus Aspects
Trine, Sextile or Conjunction

With your Moon in soft aspect to Uranus, you have a love of freedom and will want a lifestyle that doesn't bog you down in too much routine or domesticity. This aspect helps you naturally balance independence with intimacy, as long as you allow yourself to be honest about your inner emotional life.

In childhood, you may have had to learn emotional independence due to the inconsistency of caregivers. In your adult relationships, you can be very responsive to loved ones because your natural objectivity lets you see many sides to an issue. You feel unrestricted in the ways you show love to others, or in how to respond to requests for support. Your unlimited source of ideas makes you a very helpful, if somewhat erratic, friend.

To work with this soft aspect, you have to learn how to deal with any ambiguity you feel around relationships. You will most likely thrive in unconventional living arrangements and should give yourself opportunities to experience your desire for community connection. With this aspect, it is as if the whole world is your family, and yet you have to exert some effort in order to make sure that your own need for security doesn't play second fiddle to these high ideals. Taking time to acknowledge the energy of your Moon by Sign will help you see the pathway to a future of real choice and freedom.

Moon to Uranus Aspects
Square, Opposition and Conjunction

With the Moon in challenging aspect to Uranus, you may feel conflicted about your desire for relationship and your desire for freedom. With this placement, you are working to consciously provide the space for your own needs, ideas and dreams without sacrificing the treasures of truly bonding with other human beings. This requires cultivating the capacity for objective thought about yourself and those you love. Relationships are not an easy place to be objective – we are emotionally attached and stubborn about our needs.

Your early relationships with caregivers may have been fraught with chaos and devoid of real emotional intimacy. You may have perceived from an early age that you can either have loving, nurturing relationships or you can have your own fulfilling life. In your adult relationships, you are learning how to shed restless habits developed in early childhood. You may need to find an unconventional lifestyle to suit your independent streak. Just be realistic about what kind of commitment you can make to others, whether it's a friend, a child or a lover. Snap judgments or empty rebellion can derail your potential for vision and cooperation.

This lesson holds tremendous healing potential. In our society, we are often shown images of partnership that contain inherent inequalities, making it seem that we must sacrifice our dreams for the sake of our partner, family or the social order. With Uranus and the Moon working for maximum consciousness, you have the opportunity to discover brand new forms of partnership that include everyone's unique voice and perspective. The challenge is to be unafraid of commitment while holding fast to the visions you have for your life.

Moon to Neptune Aspects
Trine, Sextile or Conjunction

With your Moon in a soft aspect with Neptune, you are naturally in tune with your feelings and demonstrate devotion and compassion in your relationships. Although at times you may struggle to define your feelings to others, you do not block the flow of expression. Your acceptance of the ups and downs of your own emotional life makes you an open, loving friend to others.

You may idealize your early childhood experiences, creating a fantastic version of your family relationships and bonding. In your adult relationships, you may be looking for the ideal person, and this could keep you from seeing what's really going on. It may be important for you to create very clear boundaries in order to protect yourself from others' projections and neediness. You also have to beware of having a subconscious expectation of being taken care of by others.

There is a tremendous potential for artistic vision and talent; it just requires that you make an effort to manifest it. Creating art or fantasy may come so naturally to you that you take it for granted. Striving for a daily practice that connects you to imagination and spirit - such as journaling, sketching or meditation - ensures that such talent doesn't stay buried. Look to your Moon Sign for the areas that might inspire you to utilize your artistic vision.

Moon to Neptune Aspects
Square, Opposition and Conjunction

Neptune is the planet of dreams, longing and the collective unconscious. With the Moon in challenging aspect to Neptune, you are working on integrating imagination and spirituality more fully into your daily life. You may have a hard time distinguishing between fantasy and reality, preferring to live in your dreams rather than tackle the business of day-to-day living. There is great potential here for artistic expression, if you can enter into your inner landscapes without getting swallowed by the ego's capacity for self-deception.

Your early childhood experiences heightened the importance of merging with another in order to feel safe. Caregivers may have been somehow "gone," whether that meant actual physical absence, mental instability or an artistic, spiritual nature. In your adult relationships, you may still be looking for that ideal Mother and desire someone or something to devote yourself to. Taking a closer look at any lingering mother issues through counseling, journaling or intuitive readings will help you create stronger boundaries in your adult life.

With the Moon and Neptune pulling on you, you are becoming conscious of deeply held desires to be rescued or to play the savior. You are learning to develop trust in your intuition so you can see what vision is and what's merely illusion. Creating a daily spiritual practice and learning more about the resources your Moon imparts can help you find a sense of magic independent of others. Find an activity that inspires wonder and gratitude, such as reading a poem, singing or dancing, and make time for it each day. With the Moon and Neptune at work, God is trying to find you in the details of your days. And she's pretty persistent.

Moon to Pluto Aspects
Trine, Sextile or Conjunction

With your Moon in soft aspect to Pluto, you are probably not afraid to plumb the depths of your own psyche. You contain the patience and perseverance to work with trauma and crisis, whether your own or other people's. You are endowed with natural insight into the underlying problems of situations, as well as with compassion for the shadow parts of our psyches.

Your early childhood experiences may have given you opportunities to develop emotional strength. In your adult relationships, you are learning how to balance privacy and intimacy. The deep feelings that you contain within you must find release, and this can be threatening to our notions of security in relationships. Instead of taking your feelings for granted, establish practices of regular sharing with your loved ones, even when you're feeling moody and dark.

With this aspect, you may carry intense feelings for the family or culture you were born into. It is therefore important that you make sure to honor your personal needs for emotional safety. Don't take on such big transformational work without committing yourself to personal healing and growth as well. To work with this aspect, provide yourself with the kind of energetic support networks you need to stay healthy, such as therapy, occult practices or anything that promotes catharsis.

Moon to Pluto Aspects
Square, Opposition and Conjunction

With your Moon in hard aspect to Pluto, your need for emotional security is constantly tugging on your strong desire to transform. This tug-of-war can propel you to seek ways to control your emotional states, but it can just as easily cause you to instinctively act out your deeply subconscious desires.

Your early childhood experiences may have been fraught with secrecy and intense emotional states. In your adult relationships, you have to learn how to take enough emotional space to feel safe while still finding the courage to trust others. This aspect has an element of karma to it, and you may well be here to help heal secrets and complexes that stretch far back in your family's lineage. You may even be drawn to working with issues around sex, death and rites of passage in the larger culture.

To work with this aspect, it is vital that you give your Moon adequate attention and still be able to let go of your feelings. The work of transformation often takes surrender. The Moon by Sign and House gives insight into what makes you feel secure, but with Pluto involved you can't cling too tightly to external attachments. You have to summon up your inner emotional strength to tackle issues, and be ready to let go so you can become someone new in an instant.

Discovering Your Inner Nature

In the heart of change, we often feel like we are falling apart. We feel confused. We feel empty. We feel sorrow. We feel growing pains. We feel lost. But in the heart of change, we are often closer to our true nature than ever before. The Moon tells us this story. It wants to help us navigate our changing lives while still honoring the essence within us. This essence, which is sometimes called *soul,* is confounding, mysterious and complex. When we are in touch with our lunar nature, we can often manage more effortlessly the great and small fluctuations of modern life. But when this inner light is out of whack, when we forget our emotional, watery nature, then it can feel like we're walking in the dark. When the inner life is ignored or repressed, the outer life suffers.

Spending time moon-gazing lets the changing light infuse us. The Moon has always been a source of inspiration, directions and wisdom. It shines when we need it most: in the heart of the dark night.

The Moon speaks to us of the hidden power and depth of feeling that reaches to the very heart of what it means to be human. When we take steps toward greater self-knowledge and nurturing, we are able to tap into our unique natural resources and give our beautiful gifts to the world.

Now that you've read more about what kind of energy your Moon holds, take the next loving step and let yourself unfold into a more natural you. This is important work. People who don't know their own hearts are easily controlled, manipulated and coerced into actions that do more harm than good. Knowing ourselves can bring healing and liberation to the whole world. Leaning into the light of the Moon means letting yourself change and be changed by your connections.

In *Letters to a Young Poet*, Rilke advises,

> "Don't search for the answers, which could not be given to you now, because you would not be able to live them. And the point is to live everything. Live the questions now. Perhaps then, someday far in the future, you will gradually, without even noticing it, live your way into the answer."

Minding the Moon

Here are some suggestions to help you keep living into the questions:

- Learn more about *The Goddess Within* as touched on in the Moon by Sign section. If it feels right to you, find a way to honor this goddess, such as making offerings or asking for more guidance from her in your life. The more you learn about your specific Lunar Goddess energy, the more you will see that power at work in your life and coming naturally through you.

- Work with setting intentions. Look over the *Dark Side* section and see which challenging parts of your Moon are ready for a change. You may set an intention to let go of old patterns or to see the gift of certain challenges. Intentions can go a long way in transforming lead into gold, but remember to be patient with yourself. A strong intention holds you in its grace, and often we can't begin to guess the ways it will change us. Use the Full Moon to release old patterns or celebrate your accomplishments. Use the New Moon to plant seeds for the future and to set realistic goals about how you can manifest your reservoir of power on a day-to-day basis.

• Practice self-love. There may be hidden desires as well as shadows uncovered when we explore the Moon in our charts. It can bring up painful memories about childhood or surprising affirmations of our inmost needs. Ask for help in healing the wounds of the past. Respect the things that make you feel comfortable as important aspects of you. What's one small step you can take to make yourself feel nurtured this week? Remind yourself of your true inner nature when you feel anxiety, doubt or disillusionment creep in.

• Journaling is a great way to track your natural cycles and changes. Experiment with keeping a journal for 28-days (one lunar cycle) and see what you discover about your own rhythms, dreams and desires. You can even forget the journal and just jot down a few words on your calendar. You'll find that you are full of very different energies depending on the Sign that the Moon is currently traveling through. With a regular writing practice, you can notice the changes in you and around you as the Moon grows to Full and wanes to New. Use these questions to spark your writing: How do I feel today? What are the ways I show love to people in my life? How do I express my inner power to others? How have I been taking care of myself? When/where do I feel completely safe and supported?

Bula Mila (Many Eyes)

Climbing to the top
of a mountain
I'm told I shouldn't visit,
breaking taboos, shouldering burdens.
I don't mean to but
once my shoes are off
there seems to be
no choice in the matter,
so I begin walking.

With hard and soft medicine
I'm beckoned
by wind and desire.
Letting go while walking
becomes a pilgrimage.
While listening to the call
and the song of her voice—
some old spirit up there—
maybe something in me,
I begin the healing.

It takes years.
Maybe a lifetime.

At the top finally,
I am really upside down.
I am in the center of a darkness,
in the emptiness of unknowing.

On top of Bula Mila
I am alone
in her home, we are
alone   singing together
alone   praying together
alone   crying together
alone   dying together
alone   laughing together.

In the curve of a crescent moon,
perched on the edge like that,
we dangle our feet in unfathomable love.

from *Persephone Rising* by Rhea Wolf

Appendix A

How to get your Natal Chart

G oing to see your local astrologer for a reading might be the best way to find out what your Moon sign is. You'll also get personal and specific insight into your whole natal chart, not just your Moon. But this book is a great place to start in beginning a journey of self-discovery.

If you can't see an astrologer, there are many websites that offer great general information about the signs, houses and planets. You can visit *www.astro.com* to get your Natal Chart printed out. You'll need your birth date, time and place to get an accurate chart. Once you enter in that data, you'll be able to access free short descriptions about the various parts of your Natal Chart. You can also buy inexpensive astrology reports from *www.tarot.com*. A portion of this book first appeared as "Your Personal Moon Report" at *www.tarot.com*. I also appreciate *www.cafeastrology.com* and Moses Siregar III's astrology site *www.astrologyforthesoul.com* for their free definitions, forecasts and lessons in astrology.

If you have any questions about the content of this book, the Moon or astrology in general, email Rhea Wolf at *rhea@turningwheelastrology.com*.

Visit *www.turningwheelastrology.com* to sign up for Rhea Wolf's free monthly forecasts and to learn more about her work.

Appendix B

Astrological Symbols and Glyphs

The Signs of the Zodiac

♈ Aries   ♎ Libra

♉ Taurus   ♏ Scorpio

♊ Gemini   ♐ Sagittarius

♋ Cancer   ♑ Capricorn

♌ Leo   ♒ Aquarius

♍ Virgo   ♓ Pisces

The Planets

☉ **Sun**: Principle of creativity, ego, will, and self-image.

☿ **Mercury:** Principle of perception and communication.

♀ **Venus:** Principle of relationship, self-worth and values.

♂ **Mars:** Principle of desire, ability to assert one's self, conflict and separation.

♃ **Jupiter:** Principle of faith, growth, meaning and expansion.

♄ **Saturn:** Principle of work, structure, commitment and obstacles or blocks.

♅ **Uranus:** Principle of freedom, rebellion and individuality.

♆ **Neptune:** The collective unconscious, dreams, confusion and fantasy, spiritual aspirations.

♇ **Pluto:** Principle of deep transformation, the unknown, power and the underworld.

Appendix C

Artwork and Artist Bios

Artwork is listed in the order in which it appears in the book and is used with permission of the artists. For more information, please contact the artists.

On the Cover: *That Which I Seek* by Andrea Galluzzo

Queen of Moons by Iris Leslie (page 7)

Shedding Her Skin by Andrea Galluzzo (page 11)

An Offering by Pomegranate Doyle (page 19)

The Doorways by Pomegranate Doyle (page 47)

Asterion by Iris Leslie (page 53)

The Light in Dark Places by Andrea Galluzzo (page 79)

Unearth by Andrea Galluzzo (page 95)

Creator by Andrea Galluzzo (page 103)

The River Worker by Pomegranate Doyle (page 113)

The Comfort by Andrea Galluzzo (page 193)

In From the Other Place by Pomegranate Doyle (page 207)

The Arrival, The Reunion by Andrea Galluzzo (page 227)

Pomegranate Doyle

Artist, ritualist, priestess, healer, teacher and psychic, Pomegranate Doyle has been painting and teaching for over 25 years. She lives, paints and teaches in Portland Oregon. You can see more of her art at **www.PomegranateDoyle.com** and you can listen to her advice Podcast (where she delves into the mysteries of life, death and beyond) at **www.AskPomegranate.com.**

Andrea Galluzzo

Andrea Galluzzo is a photographer living and working in Portland, OR. Coming from years of experience working with medium and large format cameras, she began experimenting with the digital darkroom four years ago. Her knowledge and experience with chemical printing has influenced the quality and craft of her current work that pushes the boundaries of the photographic medium. Galluzzo's work focuses on themes of transformation, growth and discovery. She is driven to create images the honor the beauty that exists in moments that challenge us. Her work has been published in numerous online and print magazine and blogs including Black and White Magazine and Underexposed. She was awarded the Ultimate Eye Foundation Grant in 2009 and has exhibited her work in group and solo shows around the country including the Camerawork Gallery, Spiva Arts Center, and Rayko Photo Center. To view more of her work please follow her on Facebook or visit her website at **www.andreagalluzzo.com**.

Iris Mae Leslie

Iris Mae Leslie is an artist living in Portland, Oregon. She has been drawing and painting all her life and praises the muses that bring her the inspiration to create. "I believe in color. I believe in pen and ink. I believe that between speech and the written word is the image: a language neither spoken nor penned, but drawn out, with line and stroke and shade--a portrait of an emotion, a map of an idea." Find her work at: **www.irisleslie.com** and **www.etsy.com/shop/BrazenMae**

Bibliography

General Astrology

Bills, Rex E. *The Rulership Book,* Macoy Publishing and Masonic Supply Co. Inc. 1971.
Casey, Caroline W., *Making the Gods Work For You,* Three Rivers Press, 1998.
Forest, Steven, *The Inner Sky,* ACS Publications, 1989.
George, Demetra, *Mysteries of the Dark Moon,* San Francisco: Harper Collins, 1990.
Greene, Liz & Sasportas, Howard, *The Luminaries: the psychology of the sun and moon in the horoscope,* York Beach, Me.: S. Weiser, 1992.
Sasportas, Howard, *The Twelve Houses,* The Aquarian Press, 1986.
Spiller, Jan, *New Moon Astrology,* Bantam Dell, 2001.

General Mythology

Graves, Robert, *Greek Myths,* London: Penguin Books, 1955.
Meade, Michael, *Fate and Destiny,* Mosaic Publishing, 2012.
Pollack, Rachel, *Seventy-Eight Degrees of Wisdom,* Thorsons of Harper Collins, 1997.
Monaghan, Patricia, *The Book of Goddesses and Heroines,* Llewellyn Publications, 1990.
Walker, Barbara, *Women's Encyclopedia of Myths and Secrets,* San Francisco: Harper Collins, 1983.
Willis, Roy, *World Mythology,* Oxford University Press, 1993.

The Story of Hina

Beckwith, Martha. *Hawaiian Mythology.* New Haven: Yale University Press, 1940.
Muten, Burleigh, *Grandmothers' Stories,* Barefoot Book, 1999.

The Story of Artemis and Actaeon

Friedman, Amy, *Artemis and Orion,* February 11, 2009, http://www.cantonrep.com/life/x1450774533/Tell-Me-a-Story-Artemis-and-Orion-a-Greek-myth, accessed March 2010

The Story of Malina and Anningan

Dickason, Dr. Olive, *Kids' Site of Canadian Heritage*, January 13, 2005, http://www.collectionscanada.gc.ca/premierescommunautes/jeunesse/021013-2071.2-e.html, accessed July 2012

Romero, Frances, *The Inuit Moon and Sun Gods, February 7, 2011,* http://www.time.com/time/specials/packages/article/0,2880 4,2046823_2046865_2046803,00.html, accessed July 2012.

Poetry and Inspiration

Lal Ded (Lalla), "The Soul Like the Moon," translated by Coleman Barks, *The Shambhala Anthology of Women's Spiritual Poetry,* edited by Aliki Branstone, Shambhala, 2002.

Macy, Joanna and Brown, Molly Young, *Coming Back to Life,* New Society Publishers, 1998.

Rilke, Rainer Maria, *In Praise of Mortality*, translated and edited by Anita Barrows and Joanna Macy, Riverhead Books, 2005.

About the Author

Rhea Wolf is a passionate student and teacher of astrology, spirituality and creativity. Her genuine desire is to help people awaken their inherent creativity, activate their authentic selves and deepen their connections to the larger world.

Rhea's work is motivated by a vision of an emerging culture based on respect, beauty, justice and relatedness. Her writing has appeared in *Alternatives Magazine, The Mountain Astrologer, hipMama* and *VoiceCatcher* to name a few. She lives in the sublimely sumptuous Pacific Northwest with the sweet rain, a loving man, and two spunky daughters.

And if you're wondering, her Moon is in Taurus in the 10th House conjunct Mars. She can be reached at rhea@turningwheelastrology.com.

For workshops, forecasts and more, visit
www.turningwheelastrology.com.

2624651R00140

Made in the USA
San Bernardino, CA
14 May 2013